Twayne's English Authors Series

Herbert Spencer

TEAS 219

Courtesy of the National Portrait Gallery

Herbert Spencer

HERBERT SPENCER

By JAMES G. KENNEDY

Northern Illinois University

TWAYNE PUBLISHERS
A DIVISION OF G. K. HALL & CO., BOSTON

First Printing

Library of Congress Cataloging in Publication Data

Kennedy, James Gettier, 1932 -
Herbert Spencer.

(Twayne's English authors series ; TEAS 219)
Bibliography: p. 157-59
Includes index.
1. Spencer, Herbert, 1820 - 1903.
B1657.K4 192 78-1338
ISBN 0-8057-6688-X

MANUFACTURED IN THE UNITED STATES OF AMERICA

Contents

About the Author

James G. Kennedy is a graduate of Kenyon College and the University of Minnesota. He has published seven critical articles in *English Literature in Transition* and *College English,* on topics ranging from the British novelist Arnold Bennett, to history and modern fiction, literary realism, the form and content of *Native Son,* and cross-cultural comparison of literature in the political East and West. The articles on Bennett are listed in the standard (Goldentree) bibliography on the modern British novel. He has also edited *Stories East and West,* 1971, a collection of fictions paired by similar subjects and drawn from the works of Lu Hsun, Isaac Babel, Yuri Kazakov, Stephen Crane, and eight other writers from the East and the West. A special interest for the last decade has been British working-class literature, 1780 to the present.

Professor Kennedy's interest in Herbert Spencer began in 1957 with a freshman student's term paper on Social Darwinism. Finding that Spencer had been a strong influence on Arnold Bennett, Kennedy worked out that connection in a doctoral dissertation, "Literary Convention and the Realistic novels of Arnold Bennett," University of Minnesota, 1961. He spent a semester's leave in Cambridge, England, in 1967, for further research on Spencer, and a second semester's leave in 1975 in writing the first draft for Twayne's English Authors Series.

Professor Kennedy has been a college teacher for twenty years. Since in that time he has read widely and has taught courses in diverse fields, he can sympathize, as a literary generalist, with Spencer's enterprise as a generalist of the sciences. Kennedy has taught technical writing, the history of the English language, the structure of modern English, Victorian prose, Victorian poetry, the English novel, the nineteenth and twentieth-century European novel, surveys of Oriental, Western European, Eastern European, English, and American literature, introductions to fiction and poetry, honors seminars in Faulkner, Henry James and T. S. Eliot, the Twenties, and the Radical American Novel, and honors tutorials on Faulkner, T. S. Eliot, Thomas Hardy, Abraham Lincoln's prose, and Martin Andersen Nexö.

Preface

Herbert Spencer is known as the arch-Social Darwinist: the man who opposed any political interference with the individual's adaptation to his or her society, and who advocated that every adult should accept and suffer the consequences of his or her nature and activity. The leading idea of this study of Spencer's system of philosophy is that he underestimated the creative, social potentialities of men and women. Yet his works offer original insights, and the errors in his philosophy are so apparent today that they are comfortably cautionary.

Spencer's claim was that he was right, and for awhile and for some his claim seemed valid. But even in his lifetime, Spencer was judged to be incorrect on point after point. Today attention to his works must be like one's interest in an outmoded encyclopedia. One goes to Spencer not expecting to find what is right, but rather to review errors that were plausible a century ago. Studying Spencer means recognizing his errors. He was neither a creator of fictions nor a great philosopher. Not an artist, he does not invite suspension of disbelief, so that his reader may perceive truistic human potentialities. Not a profound thinker, he does not face fundamental issues without logical errors, so that a reader need admire the thought even while he disagrees with it. What Spencer's works still do is admonish all general writers, including the present reviewer, to be circumspect.

Chapter 1 gives some account of the origins of Spencer's mental habits and presuppositions. It traces his educational ideas to his father's example and his political ideas to his uncle's practice. It also touches on Spencer's ill-health and on the usefulness of his friendships, which lightened his spirits and advanced his career. Chapter 2 reviews his prose style. Then there follow reviews of his work in seven fields: Chapter 3, metaphysics; 4, philosophy of mind; 5, ethics; 6, biology; 7, sociology; 8, economics and political philosophy. The order of Chapters 3 - 8 reflects key relations between components of Spencer's philosophy. His metaphysics underlay his psychology, and his psychology, his ethics; biology was to be a prerequisite for both the study of sociology and a valid political philosophy. Since Spencer wrote multi-volume introductions to diverse fields of study, his long works are summarized and criticized part by part. Moreover, since Spencer was active in all of these fields for fifty years, Chapters 3 - 8 also relate his essays to his major works. Chapter 9 outlines Spencer's reputation with nineteenth-century audiences and gives special attention to his literary influence.

It has not been possible to study firsthand Spencer's reputation in non-English-speaking countries. Letters not quoted in *An Autobiography* or in David Duncan's *The Life and Letters of Herbert Spencer* have not been traced. Spencer's letters ought to be collected in the near future. Tabular evidence for the conclusions about Spencer's prose style in Chapter 2 and analyses of typical paragraphs can be obtained from the present writer.

Winona Ann Saunders Kennedy, my wife, has given me constant encouragement. Samuel Huang, Inter-Library Loan Librarian, Northern Illinois University, has located dozens of needed titles. Two research leaves—from Upsala College and from Northern Illinois University—have freed me to study Spencer: in England during the spring of 1967, and in Illinois during the spring of 1975. In 1977, J. Truslow of Boston University suggested major improvements in the manuscript and corrected many errors. I am responsible for what remains.

JAMES G. KENNEDY

DeKalb, Illinois

Chronology

1820 Herbert Spencer born, April 27, at Derby.
1833 Went to live at Hinton Charterhouse with his uncle, the Reverend Thomas Spencer.
1836 Finished three years' study of mathematics and mechanics with Uncle Thomas.
1837 Began work as a railway civil engineer under his father's pupil, Charles Fox.
1842 Visited uncle; wrote "On the Proper Sphere of Government" for *The Nonconformist;* joined uncle in work for the Complete Suffrage Union.
1843 Studied and wrote on phrenology and on literary style; sought a literary career in London.
1844 Worked on *The Pilot,* Birmingham, for Joseph Sturge (C.S.U.); returned to railway surveying.
1846 Arranged manufacture of one of his inventions, a paper clip.
1848 Introduced by uncle to James Wilson, editor of *The Economist;* became sub-editor.
1851 *Social Statics;* became friendly with George Henry Lewes and Marian Evans (George Eliot); agreed to write for Chapman's *Westminster Review.*
1852 Met Thomas Henry Huxley; "The Development Hypothesis," "A Theory of Population," "The Philosophy of Style."
1854 "The Art of Education"; "The Genesis of Science"; "Railway Morals and Railway Policy."
1855 July, began to feel tired; *The Principles of Psychology.*
1857 "Progress: Its Law and Cause"; "Transcendental Physiology"; *Essays, First Series.*
1858 "A System of Philosophy"; "The Nebular Hypothesis"; asked John Stuart Mill about a post in India Office.
1859 "What Knowledge is of most Worth?" Rpt. *Education,* 1861.

1860 "The Social Organism." Rpt. *Essays,* Revised Edition, 1890, I.
1861 *Education: Intellectual, Moral, and Physical.*
1862 *First Principles.*
1863 *Essays, Second Series.*
1864 *The Principles of Biology,* I; X Club founded.
1866 Read only experimental study to the Linnean Society, "On Circulation and the Formation of Wood in Plants"; heir on his father's death intestate.
1867 *The Principles of Biology,* II; *Descriptive Sociology* begun.
1868 Elected to Athenaeum Club; toured Italy.
1870 *The Principles of Psychology,* Second Edition, I, brought out to establish his priority.
1872 *The Principles of Psychology,* Second Edition, II.
1873 *The Study of Sociology;* "Replies to Criticisms."
1874 *Essays, Third Series;* refused nomination to Royal Society.
1876 *The Principles of Sociology,* I, Parts I - III.
1879 *The Principles of Sociology,* II, Part IV; *The Principles of Ethics,* I, Part I, "The Data of Ethics."
1882 Led Anti-Aggression League; *The Principles of Sociology,* II, Part V, "Political Institutions"; visited the U.S.
1884 *The Man 'versus' the State.*
1885 *The Principles of Sociology,* III, Part VI.
1886 Began invalidism; "The Factors of Organic Evolution."
1889 Completed *An Autobiography.*
1890 Disputes with Huxley and Weismann.
1891 *The Principles of Ethics,* II, Part IV, "Justice."
1892 *The Principles of Ethics,* I, Parts II - III.
1893 "The Inadequacy of Natural Selection"; *The Principles of Ethics,* II, Parts V - VI; dispute with Henry George.
1896 *The Principles of Sociology,* III, Parts VII - VIII.
1899 "The Filiation of Ideas."
1902 Nominated for Nobel Prize for Literature.
1903 Died December 8.

CHAPTER 1

A Fortunate Man

WHEN a man has written 400,000 words about himself, there is need for interpretation. Herbert Spencer not only could not see himself as others did, but he also seemed unaware of some of the elementary implications of his life. After a short sketch of his life, the sage will become more approachable, more human, through consideration of his mentors: his father and his uncle.

William George Spencer, the father, was a respected teacher in Derby. Although he and his wife, Harriet Holmes Spencer, had nine children, only their eldest son survived: Herbert, born on 27 April 1820. In 1833, George Spencer took his thirteen-year-old son to study with Thomas Spencer, the uncle, who was a Cambridge M.A., a reformer of the Church of England, a lecturer and writer for temperance and the New Poor Law, and a parson at Hinton Charterhouse in Somersetshire five miles south of Bath. After three years with Uncle Thomas, Herbert began work as a railway engineer. At twenty-two, he wrote his first work, *On the Proper Sphere of Government*. At twenty-eight, he received light, remunerative work as a sub-editor of *The Economist*, a London weekly that advocated free trade and an end to government regulation. In this job he had time to write his first book, *Social Statics*, which appeared when he was thirty-one. Within the next two years, he became friendly with Marian Evans (George Eliot), Thomas Henry Huxley, and John Tyndall, and became a regular contributor to the *Westminster Review*.

Herbert Spencer was literally fortunate in his family. His father and two paternal uncles made him their heir: Uncle Thomas, in 1853; Uncle William, a schoolmaster in Derby, in 1860; and George Spencer, in 1866. The first legacy enabled Herbert to devote his full time to developing his theories of evolution. Although his health broke down, he completed *The Principles of Psychology* in 1855. In 1860, he sought subscribers to his plan of work, "A System of Philosophy." Uncle William's bequest enabled him to continue the publication of the first volume of his philosophy, *First Principles*. The inheritance from his father enabled Spencer to publish the second volume of *The Principles of Biology* in 1867.

In the last three decades of his life, Spencer completed his system. In the 1870's, he published a revision of *The Principles of Psychology* (1870, 1872), *The Study of Sociology* (1873), his most profitable book, and parts of the fourth and fifth works in his system, *The Principles of Sociology* and *The Principles of Ethics*. In his last two decades, despite increasing invalidism, Spencer dictated the remaining parts of the latter two titles. He finished his autobiography in 1889 and was nominated for the Nobel Prize for Literature in 1902, a year before he died.

I *His Father*

Since he had his father's example to admire, Herbert Spencer might have become a private teacher. It had been a profession of Spencer males for two generations. A grandfather had established the second-best school in Derby and had set to work three of his sons: William George, Thomas, and William. William George, Herbert's father, became highly successful at giving private lessons and acquired the patronage of one noble house and several professional families in Derby. In his teaching, he emphasized what today would be called rapport, relevance, classroom demonstrations, problem-solving, and independent study. In achieving sympathy and sometimes a first-name basis with his pupils, he spent much time discussing religious, moral, and political ideas. In giving instruction, he aimed at practice in analysis and independence of action and thought. For stimulating mastery of geometry, he produced brain-teasers. For astronomy, physics, and chemistry, he set up instructive pieces of apparatus for the students to manipulate. For botany and zoology, he advocated collecting and drawing specimens from nature. In the early nineteenth century, these highly unusual teaching procedures brought William George Spencer fame and fortune in his city. When he married, prudently at twenty-nine, he was honorary secretary of the Derby Philosophical Society (founded in 1783 by Erasmus Darwin) and had saved several thousand pounds.[1]

When Herbert tried three months of school teaching in 1837, he also had success using his father's methods. He relied on sympathy rather than authority, he adjusted instruction to the mental development of the students, and he invented examples to make attention pleasurable. Later in life, he first became known to an international audience through a little book of four essays—*Education: Intellectual, Moral, and Physical* (1861)—in which he systematized his father's ideas without acknowledgment.[2] He dreamed of starting a school to carry out his ideas. He wanted physical education for both boys and girls, moral education that would encourage self-governance through self-help, and education in science as the study most practical for life and most effective for the discipline of intellect and feeling.[3] In 1848 he reconnoitered possibilities in Bath for setting up school with his father or for teaching mathematics there himself (I, 371).[4] But he never taught an hour after November, 1837.

Herbert Spencer never became a teacher, partly because he also had his father's example to avoid. William George Spencer had begun to give lessons when a boy, and after twenty years' teaching by his own demanding methods he found that his nervous system had become unreliable. When he gave up regular teaching in 1824, he wrote his brother Thomas, "I am still more convinced than ever that I shall never continue healthy with my present employment—the stooping, the confinement, the sameness, the trial of temper and patience that it constantly affords. . . . I do not intend to teach any more if I can obtain a living in any other way" (D, 8). He could not, and so he continued to teach part-time for forty years. The boy Herbert did not fail to notice that teaching, which had made his father respectable, had also drained him emotionally and had given him an excuse for perfectionist behavior. His much-emulated father let himself become an irritable martinet at home who could never decide that his two books, on shorthand and geometry, were complete. His dictatorial attitude and coldness to Herbert's mother—who bore four other boys and four girls—may also have influenced his only son to remain a bachelor. At twenty-four, Herbert warned his best friend, who was about to marry, against a relationship where the man dominates and degrades the woman (I, 307).

Yet Spencer regarded himself as a lesser man than his father, intellectually, emotionally, and physically (I, 48). A handsome man who had remarkable presence, George Spencer could afford to disapprove of all social bonding that results from deference. He tolerated ranks, honors, and privileges; but he talked persuasively against them and ignored them personally in order to hasten their abolition. In the pre-Reform county town of Derby, he would take off his hat to no person, would use no titles except "Mr." and

"Mrs.," and recognized no religious authority. And no one took offense at Mr. George Spencer.

Unquestionably his son had regrets, however, for the ways in which his father was conventional. He had had an ascetic upbringing as a Methodist, objected to theater-going, and disapproved of fiction, which his son dearly loved (I, 87, 120). He was not a hearty Dickensian man, ready to give and take pleasure, but austere and prone to be contentious and harsh. At forty he started attending Sunday morning meetings of the Friends, to feel free from the direction of a minister and congregation; but with him he took Herbert, who also had to attend Methodist chapel with his mother on Sunday evenings. The son later declared himself ignorant of any effect, except a dislike for all Biblical expressions, and implied that his father was essentially a deist, a supporter of natural religion based on reason, rather than a believer in revelation (I, 94, 101; D, 80). But Herbert Spencer, John Stuart Mill remarked, was "as anti-clergymanish as possible"; and he dearly loved a joke on revelation (II, 424).[5] It is unlikely that his irritable, high-minded father would have shared his son's amusement. George Spencer knew and quoted the Bible and hoped that by "a holy use of his present knowledge . . . [his son would] be led into all truth" (I, 655). According to the father, *Social Statics* resulted from his challenge to his son to try to write a better book on ethics than the father's favorite account of Christian ethics (I, 351). And when the son dealt directly with that ethic thirty years later, he cited only the obscure work that his father had favored: a sign not only of affection for his father, but also of indifference bred by a month of Sundays from 1830 to 1833.[6]

The son later felt the most gratitude for the facilities for learning to which he had had access in his home. Periodicals came from the Philosophical Society's library, the Methodist library, and the Mechanics' Institute. He could listen to discussions on learned subjects that his father encouraged among the uncles and other visitors. His father put apparatus for physical and chemical experiments at his disposal. There were specimens at hand in the large garden and the fields and hedgerows beyond it. As for direct instruction, the son felt that his father both neglected and reproached him too often. It was annoying that his father habitually gave his pupils more time than they paid for and even gave free evening lessons to promising working-class youths. His father seemed to have left over for his son only frail health and low energy (I, 57, 92).

Yet George Spencer gave his son gifts of time and energy that Herbert Spencer never adequately acknowledged. When Herbert felt jubilant at twenty for his inventiveness at his engineering work, he heard from his father about "the never-ceasing pains taken . . . in early life," to develop his "inventive powers" (I, 190). The son was only conscious that he had not been forced to learn, that he had not read well until he was seven, and that his father had often said, "As usual, Herbert, thinking only of one thing at a time" (I, 86). He never connected his manner of thinking—a policy of never puzzling himself but, instead, waiting for years for a theory to develop itself in his mind—with his father's method of watchful, always receptive waiting. His father was his faithful, always interested correspondent for thirty-three years, from 1833 to 1866. But the son congratulated, not his father, but himself for his 'castle-building" and for his unlined forehead (I, 85, 462 - 64).[7]

Spencer also never realized two shortcomings of his father's mentorship. First, though he became a thinker and a writer, he never became a reader. Impatient with any book, he would not read one whose premises he could not accept (I, 289). As a result, he never was taken by a "current of thought to the opposite side of the question," as Matthew Arnold proposed might well be the course of a thinker.[8] Kant and Marx, let alone classical and medieval thinkers, need never have written, since he could determine from reading fifty pages, or even a summary, that he would reject their premises. The books that he did read and receive stimulus from were more often than not textbooks—standard, but not primary works. When Grant Allen visited him in 1876, he was dictating in a book-lined workroom; but he used the books for reference, not for reading.[9] One can admire Herbert Spencer's pleasure at solving a theorem on circles at twenty and publishing his demonstration as one hitherto unnoticed. Yet it is disconcerting to find that Plato had solved that theorem two thousand years before (I, 187, 606).[10] One feels, indeed, that Plato's precedence would not have much disturbed him.

Second, his delight in his own intuitions, nurtured in him by his father, did not teach him circumspection. It became most important to him that his theories should seem complete. Although he advocated the study of science, he mastered no field of any science and performed only one series of experiments in his life. As a result, he never disciplined himself, like Huxley and Darwin, to reserve judgment in the absence of trustworthy evidence or to respect expert opinion (I, 591).[11] Instead, he felt that "leaving a truth in an inductive form is, in a sense, leaving its parts with loose ends, and bringing it to a deductive form is, in a sense, uniting its facts as all parts of one fact" (D, 535). Everyone knows Huxley's quip that Spencer's notion of a plot for a tragedy was "the slaying of a beautiful deduction by an ugly fact" (D, 502; I, 467). Huxley read the page proofs of *The Principles of Biology* and *An Autobiography* in order to save Spencer from error, but could not persuade him that adequate evidence was lacking for his earliest theory, the inheritance of acquired characteristics (D, 270). Because that theory was essential to the completeness of his system, it had to be defensible and true.

II *Uncle Thomas*

In July, 1833, William George Spencer took his thirteen-year-old son from Derby to Hinton Charterhouse near Bath, so that the Reverend Thomas Spencer might tutor his nephew in mathematics and languages. Perhaps the father hoped that his brother would be able to prepare Herbert for his own college, St. John's, Cambridge, but from the first the boy would not apply himself to learning the necessary Latin and Greek. He found himself left by his suave, if feeble father with a firm, energetic uncle, who seemed determined to keep him in his bedroom all winter to study Latin grammar (D, 13). Ten days later, on August 1, 1833, the boy ran away to walk the one hundred and thirty miles home, the distance from Bath to Derby (I, 106 - 09). Running and walking ninety-five miles in two days, he was home on the third day, sick and terrified at his disobedience. He returned to his uncle, however, for three years, with summer vacations at home, during which time Thomas persevered in teaching what he thought Herbert required: the " 'Fear of the Lord' " and the "fear of Parents, Tutors, etc," mathematics, Newton's first book, and some Latin, Greek, and French (I, 119).

Encouraged in theorizing by his father, the son received from his uncle practice in study, argument, and politics. Although he was an ascetic, non-deferential, argumentative martinet like the father, Thomas Spencer was several things new to the son: a Churchman, a disciplinarian, an active Radical lecturer, and a bore. He could tell his hostess at a party where his nephew was not waltzing, "No Spencer ever dances," and he could converse only of the cause that he currently advocated (I, 31). But without the Reverend Thomas Spencer's tutoring and his recommendations, Herbert might have become a teacher like his father, rather than first a civil engineer and then a journalist. Without the example of his uncle's twenty-three pamphlets, which averaged sales of ten thousand copies, and of his uncle's frequent trips to speak on temperance, it is doubtful whether *The Proper Sphere of Government* and *Social Statics* would have appeared in print. The nephew developed his first political and economic ideas in controversy with Uncle Thomas, ideas which he modified only slightly in the succeeding fifty years of his life. The childless uncle developed a "semi-paternal feeling" for his older brother's son, whose talents were "of a very superior order" (I, 396, 119). He enlisted him in support of his own causes and rewarded him with introductions to men of influence.

According to his nephew's and his brothers' estimate of him on his death in 1853, Uncle Thomas was a hard man (I, 38, 373). Although he had suggested the name "Herbert" for his nephew by having sent home from college in 1819 the churchyard poem by Herbert Knowles, Thomas Spencer might have forgotten by 1833 the sympathy that he had once felt for the humble Knowles, who had died before he could complete his preparation for University study (I, 72; D, 7).[12] Thomas Spencer had worked hard as a teacher to get the money to attend St. John's, where by more hard work he had received an honors degree: ninth wrangler, 1820. His own success and prosperity had persuaded him that good conduct would always guarantee prosperity and that failure was, in every case, the result of misconduct. He gave indignant exercise to his moral sentiments when Herbert ran away from him and had to be reminded by George Spencer of the intense homesickness he had shown while at work away from their father before going on to Cambridge. Thomas Spencer was not successful in teaching his nephew, who resented his rule, to be a scholar; but he brought him on in geometry and trigonometry and set him to reading aloud Harriet Martineau's *Tales of Political Economy*.

Equally important were the daily discussions of the uncle's reform activities. In 1833, he was applying the New Poor Law in his parish, Hinton Charterhouse, reducing the poor rates from £700 to £200 a year. In 1835, he became the first Chairman of the Board of Guardians of the Bath workhouse. Herbert, set to proofreading his uncle's pamphlets, was writing to the press himself before long in defense of the New Poor Law. An Evangelical at Cambridge, the uncle had already offended his bishop by his views on Church reform, revision of the prayer book, separation of church and state, and national education. After his nephew left his house in 1836, he began to agitate for the repeal of the Corn Laws and for universal male suffrage.

Meanwhile, he had placed his student as a civil engineer on a railway, under one of George Spencer's former pupils. Herbert then had three gratifying years discovering his real superiority to most of his peers, including members of "the ruling classes," who were University graduates or had service "connexions" (I, 159 - 60). His refusal of permanent employment as an engineer of locomotives (a mechanical engineer) saved him from the fate of a functionary: lifelong overwork to keep trains running on the company schedule. His reasons were not only that the man whom he would have replaced had just been scalded to death on the job; he disapproved of his boss's pressure on his staff to spend sixteen hours a day to produce the plans for a Cornish railway (I, 209 - 10). His sense of justice overruled the security in view and his loyalty to his chief. It was his uncle who had shown him the duty of acting on a sense of justice.

When the young man later visited his uncle in 1842, they became well pleased with each other. In daily talks they found that they shared kindred political views—in fact the views of Dissent and of shopocracy and millocracy. Uncle Thomas was one of the small minority in the Church of England who cooperated with Dissenters—all of the religious groups refusing to conform to the Established Church. J. D. Y. Peel has traced the intellectual and social bases of the Spencers' community of views: support for laissez-faire economics and for freedom of worship; antagonism to the state church, to national education, and to legislative meddling.[13] The nephew emphasized a "self-adjusting principle" in society, whereas the uncle expressed "an unqualified belief in the sufficiency of self-help." But they shared "a common tendency towards Individualism" (I, 372, 238).[14] The nephew took up his uncle's suggestion to write a series of letters on politics for the Reverend Edward Miall, his uncle's acquaintance, who for a year had been publishing a militant Dissenting newspaper, *The Nonconformist*.

The uncle's stimulus may have entered most into letters IV and IX. In IV, Herbert cited the theologian William Paley on the expedient—the beneficial in collateral and remote, as well as immediate effects—without having read Paley, but Uncle Thomas would have read Paley at Cambridge (D, 418).[15] In letter IV, Herbert also voiced the prescientific view that mental derangement, bodily disease, or temporal want "were the sins of the wicked . . . visited upon the children to the third and fourth generation." Poverty in a well governed country—though not in misgoverned England after the terrible winter of 1842—would be as his uncle said, the result of misconduct.[16] From his own reading in late 1840 about the theories of J. B. Lamarck, the nephew brought in his own views on the inheritance of a tendency to morality, an acquired trait, and on the modification of organs and instincts through disuse. But it is possible that the visitation of sins remained with him as a subconscious association supportive of his dogmatic belief in the inheritance of acquired traits (I, 201).[17]

In letter IX, the nephew defended suffrage for the working classes on the ground that they could safely direct a legislature which properly restricted its legislation to the administration of justice.[18] Suffrage for working men was a topic close to his uncle's heart in May, 1842, for he had just returned from meetings in Birmingham involving leaders of the Complete Suffrage Union, such as Joseph Sturge and Edward Miall, and moral-force Chartists like William Lovett and Bronterre O'Brien. That summer he founded the Bath branch of the C.S.U. with Chartist Henry Vincent; and his nephew became honorary secretary of the Derby branch, writing a protest against the magistrates' banning a lecture by Vincent in September (D, 36, I, 250).[19]

That year the uncle wore the white hat of the Radical, and the nephew, the Chartist cap. In January, an engineer friend warned Herbert that he was "radical all over," and in July Thomas Spencer was called a Chartist for an anti-government speech (I, 231; D, 35).[20] But the Plug riots of early fall made the C.S.U. more anxious to conciliate the middle, than the working classes.[21] Uncle and nephew attended a conference with the Chartists in Birmingham on December 27, and witnessed the failure of the C.S.U. tactic of substituting a "People's Bill of Rights," for which the uncle spoke, for the Charter. Eventually important for Herbert was Uncle Thomas's introduction of him to Lawrence Heyworth, who had been most antagonistic to the working-class majority, crying, "We will espouse your principles, but we will not have your leaders. . . . I say again, . . . we'll not have you—you tyrants!" (I, 251).[22] Two years later, this wealthy Liverpool merchant invited Herbert to his home, where he met Heyworth's daughter and her husband, the Richard Potters; and they, together with their five daughters, became a second family for Spencer until his death. Meanwhile, Uncle Thomas went on indefatigably to lecture in twenty towns in 1843 for the People's Bill of Rights, and Herbert went to London to seek literary notice by publishing at his own expense his letters to *The Nonconformist* as *The Proper Sphere of Government.* On the reverse of the title page, he listed nineteen of his uncle's two-penny pamphlets.

In London, he wrote "a fiery little document" for the Anti-State-Church Association; but when after six months the literary world still did not require him, and his engineering savings were gone, he retired to his home. In the summer of 1844, he received through Joseph Sturge the position of sub-editor on a new C.S.U. paper, *The Pilot,* in Birmingham. Although he had used the expression "our religion" in *The Proper Sphere of Government,* Herbert, his engineer friends, and his uncle knew that the current creed was alien to the natural laws of progress that he espoused in conversation (I, 172 - 73). The Quaker Sturge, however, was shocked to discover the rationalism of his employee and house guest and arranged new employment for him on another family project, a railway survey. One result of this slight was that Herbert intensified his free thinking. In early 1845, he was recommending Strauss's *Life of Jesus* to one friend, losing another who objected to his heterodox views, and opining that a "moral Euclid" needed to be written. He pursued news of the "development theory"—1844 had seen publication of Robert Chambers' anonymous *Vestiges of the Natural History of Creation*—and although he put in appearances at C.S.U. and temperance meetings, he disappointed his uncle by refusing to make a speech and so become further involved.

After two years divided between civil engineering and inventing, he pleased his uncle by so independently and successfully introducing liberals in Derby to the qualifications of Lawrence Heyworth, that they asked Heyworth to be their candidate for Parliament in early 1848 (I, 362). After Heyworth's election, Herbert wrote his uncle in April about his own possibilities—either emigration to New Zealand or teaching in Bath. Uncle Thomas's response was to give him a letter of introduction to James Wilson, M.P. and proprietor of *The Economist.* This was the key financial weekly for the Heyworths of England, the newly wealthy middle-class men who tended to be Unitarians in religion, laissez-faire in economics, and strong on self-help.[23] While looking into an unfortunate railway investment of his uncle's, Herbert visited Wilson's London office, was invited to tea, and left expecting a sub-editorship. He had to submit to six months' waiting—no doubt a decent interval after a general election—before he received the position his usefulness had merited above seventy applications from others (I, 378 - 7, 382 - 83). The duties were light—thirty hours a week—and he reported to his uncle that he used his leisure time for his own writing. Wilson had supposed that the young man would publish something that would be supportive of his journal's standpoint; his letter containing the offer had promised "considerable leisure to attend to any other pursuit, such as preparing a work for the press."

The discipline of being kept waiting, and yet of being expected to produce, had its effect. Spencer worked steadily and carefully on a manuscript, and it appeared in 1851 as *Social Statics*. His uncle came to live in London and showed great tolerance for his nephew's matured conviction that nothing could be affirmed or denied about a First Cause. He could be tolerant, since his nephew was retaining from *The Proper Sphere of Government* at least the language of natural religion. "The [Creator's] great design of human progression" became in 1851 a theorem in which the "divine Idea" was faint indeed: "God wills man's happiness. Man's happiness can be produced only by the exercise of his faculties. But to exercise his faculties he must have liberty to do all that his faculties naturally impel him to do. Then God intends that he should have that liberty. Therefore he has a right to that liberty."[24] As Spencer was later to declare, "merely putting at the back of immutable law [which in *Social Statics* was "adaptation to circumstances"[25]] a divine idea, practically amounts to nothing: immutable law might stand just as well by itself" (I, 415).

Many of Spencer's economic, political, and moral ideas in *Social Statics* remained unchanged from *The Proper Sphere of Government*. The only surprising thing is that a young man so much indulged, so well provided for, and so carefully advanced by his elders should write so seriously of the beneficial discipline of nature or experience.[26] The recipient of so much generosity would allow it only to victims of accidents and to men who helped themselves.[27] The man who could write casually of his own "invincible idleness" (I, 392), wrote approvingly of "the starvation of the idle and [the] shoulderings aside of the weak by the strong." From a boy of only average vigor (I, 88), there developed a man who tried many employments, became a disbeliever, and announced that "society is constantly excreting its unhealthy, imbecile, slow, vacillating, faithless members."[28] From the reformer who had sympathized with "the distresses of the people" in 1842 and who had hoped to conciliate the Chartists came the cold morality that "the improvident masses" can learn self-control only "by a sharp experience."[29]

The explanation would seem to be that his solitary upbringing and the individualistic thinking in his elders' friendship circles complemented each other, giving Spencer a blind spot about his own good fortune. It was very clear to him, in viewing others who were more privileged by birth or office, that every person was to be judged on his merits, and that "nature" must be preferred to the corrupt state which meddled with the religion and education of Englishmen and interfered with their commerce. Absorbing from his Dissenting milieu a militant disaffection for the established order, Spencer did not do justice to how much he himself depended upon and had learned and received from others.[30] He did not consider that without help from family and friends, no one could escape nature's judgment; all then would be "nature's failures."[31]

At no time did Spencer consider how much of his behavior was evoked first by others' expectations of him and then by their reactions to him as his audience. Thomas Spencer died of overwork in January, 1853, leaving his nephew a legacy of £500. By July, Herbert Spencer had left *The Economist* to give full time to his writing. In vain did he draw natural law lessons from his uncle's devotion to duty: his own health broke down two years later as he drove to finish his second book. He admitted to being a lively talker in his youth, but denied that he needed human conversation (I, 319; II, 266). Yet he always sought an interested audience for stimulation and approbation, and he was fortunate always to find one. Once it had been his father solely; then he kept his eye on his distant uncle; in 1850 he began to gather an audience in those who wrote for John Chapman's *Westminster Review*. Later, he would have the X Club and the Athenaeum Club for stimulation; and for approbation after his father's death, he made an American, Edward L. Youmans, his constant correspondent.

III *Friends and Admirers*

Across the street from *The Economist* office was John Chapman's publishing business and boarding house. Spencer had met Chapman in 1847; and in 1849 at his house he met Eliza Lynn and Barbara Leigh Smith, and in 1851, Marian Evans. After he had finished *Social Statics,* Spencer felt time on his hands and gave thought to marriage. The man of thirty whom these women saw was thin, tall for his generation, with a ruddy face displaying an aquiline nose and bold dark hazel eyes, and he wore wings of brown hair over his ears and whiskers under his chin. Except for a protruding chin and mouth and a long upper lip, his face was attractive, his voice was a clear, good bass for glee-singing, and his step was springy. Intriguingly, his hands were smaller than the hands of a woman shorter than he. In 1851 his book was selling well, and Chapman wanted him to become a contributor to *The Westminster Review.* He had become a man who could talk "right at you like a book," in "fluent and adaptive" language; and he could laugh till the tears came.[32] In 1858, Eliza Lynn married; but later Spencer requisitioned her pen in his defense and her advice, as a "Grundyometer," to avoid offending hyper-conventional, or prudish readers (D, 311, 363).[33] Barbara Leigh Smith introduced Spencer to her uncle, Octavius Smith, the owner of the largest distillery in England, whom she knew had kindred laissez-faire views. Starting in 1856, Spencer was often Smith's guest during August and September at his Argyllshire summer home. After Smith's death in 1871, Spencer continued to vacation on Loch Aline with his son, Valentine, who added yacht excursions to the fishing and shooting.

When Marian Evans took up residence at Chapman's in the fall of 1851, she and Spencer became friends, and then in 1852, constant companions (I, 457).[34] They shared common origins in Midland Dissent—her aunt and uncle had both belonged to the "Derby Faith"—and the niece and nephew had both rejected orthodox religious beliefs (I, 26 - 7).[35] He admired her intellect, her sympathy, her calmness, her voice, her smile, the shape of her head; yet he denied that he ever loved her. He encouraged her to write novels; and she apparently found some fascination in his talk, although she would not argue with him. Spencer recalled that she was disposed to disapprove of harsh judgments, to which, of course, he was prone. In May, June, and July, 1852, these two intelligent, articulate persons frequently "paced backwards and forwards for an hour or so, discussing many things," on the Thames-side terrace of Somerset House. It is an intriguing tableau: the would-be Samson who had aimed a blow at officialdom with *Social Statics,* promenading with the woman who was critical of existing institutions but who would advocate submission to the "endowed classes" who "hold the treasures of knowledge" (I, 458 - 59, 462).[36] The backdrop was Somerset House, the seat of the Poor Law Commissioners and the location soon of Dickens' Circumlocution Office.[37] Their intimacy continued, and once Miss Evans pleaded for his companionship and implied that she could love him.[38] But Spencer's evolutionary theory had gotten under way, and he had introduced George Henry Lewes to Marian Evans (D, 544, 64). Later they rationalized: she, that he lacked emotion; he, that she lacked beauty (II, 520).[39] The real obstacle may have been that Spencer was too confident to need Marian Evans, so that she never had the opportunity to try to devote herself to him as she had implied she might.[40] They remained loyal friends when she lived with Lewes and when she became Mrs. Cross. He admired her novels, and she read his books, sometimes more than once.[41]

Spencer also gained respect from his male friends, although possibly Thomas Henry Huxley, whom he had met in 1852, disappointed him by not proposing his election to the Royal Society in 1856. When Spencer refused to be a candidate for the Society in 1874, he said that he might have been, had he been asked "within a moderate time after the publication of *The Principles of Psychology* in 1855." Huxley had said that there were "grand ideas" in Spencer's psychology, but he had helped to secure the election of twenty-two-year-old John Lubbock in 1856 (D, 168 - 70, 81).[42] Nevertheless, Huxley provided Spencer with something better than a badge of honor: he included him in a dinner club of "a few of the most advanced men of science." Huxley's and John Tyndall's friends—agnostics all—formed the X Club, which first met regularly on December 1, 1864: the first Thursday of the month, two hours before the monthly Royal Society meeting. When a year later Spencer announced cessation of the publication of his "System," the Club's proposal to take up additional subscriptions anticipated even the generosity of John Stuart Mill, who offered a guarantee. George Spencer's death on April 26, 1866, brought Spencer an inheritance that enabled him to spare his friends their expense. Mourning did not prevent his attending the May 3 meeting, when the members gave each other Club names, including Xalted Huxley, Xquisite Lubbock, Xcentric Tyndall, and Xhaustive Spencer (II, 162 - 63).[43]

The X Club gave Spencer a base where he was recognized as an equal by men of science. Twice, when a Club member was President of the British Association (as occurred five times), Spencer joined the members of the Club who came to the annual meeting and shared a suite of rooms with them at the chief hotel. At Belfast in 1874, Tyndall said of Spencer, "the ganglia of this Apostle of the Understanding are sometimes the seat of a nascent poetic thrill."[44] At Club dinners, eminent scientists—for example, Charles Darwin and Wilhelm Helmholtz—met Spencer as an admired intimate of the men who were thought to govern scientific affairs. In turn, Spencer could invite Edward L. Youmans, an ardent lecturer and writer in the United States for Spencer's philosophy. In 1871, three Club members became the London Advisory Committee for Appleton's International Scientific Series, which Youmans edited, and three contributed titles to the Series.[45] In 1872, Youmans founded *The Popular Science Monthly* in order to publish Spencer's articles, beginning with the chapters of *The Study of Sociology;* and Spencer made that journal his exclusive American outlet. He jokingly wrote to Youmans, "If things go on thus, I shall make a fortune by philosophy" (D, 160q., 375).

His X Club name, "Xhaustive," suggests how among scientists and laymen in the last third of the nineteenth century, Spencer became the most influential general writer on man's place in nature. He seemed to have an encyclopedic acquaintance not only with the physical and life sciences, but also with fields of theory that have since become the social sciences. Above all, he was adept at generalizing about the unity of all knowledge. In support of Spencer's application for government service in 1858, Joseph D. Hooker and John Tyndall praised him on both scores. And Huxley went farther: he perceived Spencer's ambition to show "the mutual connexion and interdependence of all forms of cognition," and approved it as a "necessary piece of work for us" (D, 91).

The esteem which Spencer gained might seem incredible, nevertheless, until his career and his ideas are viewed in the context of the late nineteenth century. Like George Eliot and George Henry Lewes, he was a polymath in the first generation of intellectuals and scientists who were specialists. The generation that matured between 1850 and 1860 began the professionalization of work in many fields, establishing bodies of special and theoretical knowledge, standards for performance, and special societies and schools to certify workers in good standing. But most intellectual and service workers did not attain recognition for their fields as autonomous and self-regulating until the twentieth century. So, by 1860, professional organizations were small or yet to come,[46] but specialization was already producing unusual amounts of information. Readers were not yet reconciled to being generally ignorant of fields outside their work or study and were still hopeful, in Huxley's words, of getting coordination of accumulated data. Spencer benefited from both situations. Professional experts had not yet the acknowledged authority to rule him out of court, and not all scientists were put off by the impression he made of being omniscient.[47]

The place of Spencer's ideas in nineteenth-century thought about man in relation to nature has been indicated by Robert M. Young, whose essays will be cited in many of the following chapters.[48] On the one hand, Spencer's ideas, like Mill's and Huxley's, were contributions to free thought. In the spirit of the X Club, they were "untrammeled by religious dogmas."[49] But that did not mean that his views fell foul of English ideology. Rather, from Adam Smith through Thomas Malthus and the Utilitarians (Bentham and the Mills) to the evolutionists, there was a continuous celebration of uniform, self-acting laws of nature. Natural theology, like William Paley's proof for an all-powerful and good God through evidences (like the human eye) of a Creator's design, might give way before geological evidence; but natural 'laws' had been readied to provide evidences of a secular providence for industrial society.[50] There were Smith's law of supply and demand, Malthus' law of population, and the political economists' law of the natural identity of interests.[51] Spencer contributed a law justifying the competition of unequals (the law of equal freedom) and another (use-inheritance) guaranteeing slow progress and rationalizing hierarchical division of labor in both physiology and society.[52]

So, on the other hand, Spencer's great reputation in the 1870's and 1880's was firmly based on an assumption that had been widely accepted for a century: the uniformity of nature even in social and political phenomena.[53] His plausible theories as to the mechanisms of biological evolution promised very gradual social progress through adaptation to inequality and to painful, individual struggle for existence.[54] Even adversaries—theologians, idealists, Utilitarians—would not question his ideological soundness: he meant no harm to their social order. All in all, Spencer's ideas "made sense" in ways that seemed familiar, acceptable, and useful.

IV *One of Nature's Failures*

It is touching that after 1855 Spencer regarded his own health as frail, since he had claimed that it was a natural law that unhealthy members of a society would die. Consistently, he regarded his nervous condition as the result of his own bad conduct—over-working. The pattern of good conduct in Spencer's ethics was the "healthy man of high powers," Richard Potter, whom he had admired for his genial, expansive disposition and good looks ever since they had met in 1845 (I, 298; D, 492).[55] Spencer never expected to outlive Potter, but he did, by almost twelve years. The story of Spencer's progressive illness is very sad and reminiscent of other courses of chronic ill-health by other Victorian intellectuals.

After hiking in the Alps in August, 1853, Spencer had begun to have heart palpitations. In July, 1855, a feeling in his head—apparently one of tiredness, since it was not one of pain, fever, or tension—interrupted the writing of his psychology. Thereafter, although never disinclined or unable to think or write, he had to limit his work and kill time to get to sleep at night. He had always experienced chilliness, but sleeplessness and the fear of not being able to work at all led him to reduce his daily working time to hours, and after 1886, to minutes.[56] One explanation that he gave for his difficulties—overwork—is incredible in the light of his habitual idleness. His father had worked too hard and had suffered from headaches and then an upsetting combination of physical ills and extreme irritableness. That example and, no doubt, his father's advice encouraged him to accuse himself of overdoing. But as his father's symptoms did not appear, he adopted another account: congenital deficiency in the development of his lungs and major blood vessels (II, 500 - 01).

It is possible that Spencer's symptoms were the effects of one or more of the toxic drugs available from chemists and approved by the medical profession during the 1880's.[57] But the chief fact is that he made opium his regular sedative, building from an occasional use of morphine in the 1860's to one and a half grains of opium nightly in the 1890's. Although he had seen his father die from an overdose of morphine, he dismissed doctors' advice as unduly fearful and became a habitual user of a narcotic that may have gradually enfeebled him.[58]

Spencer did not see himself as one of the "silly people" whom he would not protect from the ill effects of their "putting faith in empirics." He did not call himself one of "nature's failures," since he was "sufficiently complete to live," felt little pain, and enjoyed keen senses, good friends, and work that he both wished to do and brought to completion.[59] His disorder justified a multitude of shifts: unable to read for long, he had an excuse for asking for others' information; unable to work, he could play racquets, tennis, and billiards, and go fishing; unable to sleep, he could daydream. Having his health to preoccupy him, both the brief elation of publication and the continual vexation with critics could become bygones (II, 534 - 35).[60] His last days, as he wrote Beatrice Potter Webb, were spent day-dreaming of "coincidences," and "the average colour of the whole consciousness produced [was] grey" (D, 471).[61] Even had a determined woman found and married this English Spinoza of Market Street, he, like Isaac B. Singer's philosopher, would still have gladly communed with his stars: his pulse and the barometer.[62]

CHAPTER 2

Prose Style

FINDING that his style was "lucid," but that it had a "monotony" displeasing to him, Herbert Spencer was fair to himself.[1] Other views ranged from Mark Twain's—"Spencer could unwind a thought . . . smoothly and orderly," in "clean, clear, crisp English"—to Vernon Lee's: [Spencer was] "incapable of raising [his] feet so as to clear a single step" of an argument.[2] Surprise, at least, was one turn never used and one effect never intended by Spencer, who aimed always at a symmetrical result. Through practice, he developed variety and emphasis sufficient to meet his own criteria for an efficient style. The result is pedestrian, calm, and entertaining for the illusion of omniscience that it generates. His best moments, for the modern reader, occur when Spencer offers telling analogies.

Although it is fair, Grant Allen's estimate must be interpreted: ". . . Spencer's style, both in speech and writing was one of the most highly elaborated and perfectly adapted instruments ever invented by a human brain for a particular purpose. It did all that was wanted of it with admirable force, precision, and economy."[3] Spencer had a realistic conception of his literary abilities. He knew that a fine style was beyond his reach, but he worked to give his sentences variety and vigor.[4] Following a simple conception of language, he made his writing a perfectly adequate instrument to present generalizations and examples dispassionately.

I *Practice*

Dominating the style of *The Proper Sphere of Government* (1843) are the *passive* and the *that* transformations, as in this sentence: "In the same manner, it must *be remembered,* that although an established education, may, for a time, stimulate the national mind into a rapid growth, we must not therefore presume, *that* its results will not *be* ultimately far *surpassed* by those of the natural system."

Comparison shows that Spencer used fifteen and twenty-nine percent more *passive* and *that* transformations in his first work than he did in four later works.[5] Spencer's view that his writing was monotonous can be explained to some extent by his rather heavy use of the passive transformation. Both in main and in subordinate clauses, Spencer tended to include more passive verbs than it was Matthew Arnold's or Thomas Henry Huxley's practice to do.

In later years, Spencer's increasing efforts to introduce variety into his writing took the form of setting back subjects from the beginnings of sentences. The many introductory elements produce a gliding, nerveless effect. They weaken what force Spencer's active verbs might have gained from the stress a reader naturally brings to the beginning of any sentence. By a winding course, the reader can find the main clause, which trails off into a subordinate clause or a participial phrase rather than receiving the normal strong stress of the sentence ending.[6] While Spencer's procedure thus loses opportunities for emphasis, it does gain evenness from levelling the beginning, middle, and end of each sentence. Spencer noticed that after he began to dictate his writing in 1859, his style seemed to become more "diffuse." He mistook for looseness the blandness produced by increased numbers of sentence beginnings which diverted stress from subjects. A paragraph in *The Study of Sociology*, Spencer's most popular book, ended as follows:

> Without dwelling on the important deductions from this great truth made by Sir W. Thomson, Rankine, Tyndall, and others, I will merely draw attention to its highly-abstract nature as again showing the baselessness of the above-quoted notion.[7]

In comparison with forceful sentences by Macaulay, Arnold, or Huxley, Spencer's sentences are flat, if not dull. But they always seem balanced, even when they wobble. It is smoothness and steadiness that produces Spencer's illusion, which Henry Michel observed, of limpidity, of letting facts speak for themselves.[8]

II *Theory*

In the same year that he was revising the text of *The Proper Sphere of Government*, Spencer wrote his first draft for "The Philosophy of Style" (1852), which he called "The Force of Expression."[9] When he was writing *Social Statics* (1849 - 50), this essay prompted him to revise his manuscript twice. The essay was an original theory of effective English sentences, and was arrived at after readings in rhetoricians' handbooks. It warned him away from over-dependence on a few kinds of phraseology, the too limited style of *The Proper Sphere of Government.*[10]

But "The Philosophy of Style" also gave him the principle for his practice of proliferating beginnings of sentences. The essay shows that he had the misconception very early that a reader would be spared misunderstandings and could conserve energy, if all embedded elements in sentences, and even parts of the basic English sentence pattern, preceded the main subject and verb.[11] He advocated not only that participial phrases and subordinate clauses would be easier to read at the beginnings of sentences, but also that auxiliaries, complements, and objects would be easier to grasp if placed before the subject. The reader—by having to carry forward toward the subject all qualifications of it, providing that they were not too many—would apprehend the subject unmistakably with least trouble and so with most force (342, 345 - 47). *Paradise Lost,* accordingly, was exemplary of this most "direct" style. Persons of strong memory and concentration would prefer it, while the "indirect" or "natural" style was used by the common people, who had "undisciplined minds" (348). Two difficulties with Spencer's theory of forcible expression are, first, that he overlooked the beginning and ending stresses in English sentences, which can greatly aid a reader in grasping subjects that come first and other nouns that come last; and secondly, that he supposed that abnormal sentence patterns could be more natural for anyone than normal patterns (e.g., Subject + Verb + Object(s) + Adverbials). These oversights would be merely quaint had Spencer not sought to apply his theory of forcible expression against the grain of the language.

Spencer's theory also involved a fundamental misconception of language in general. Although not so crude as his 1843 view "that language is but a channel for the communication of knowledge," his later notion was of a simple correspondence of "a mechanical apparatus" of written symbols to the thinking of both writer and reader (335).[12] A "mode of expression" ideally would correspond to the same "state of feeling" in both the writer and the reader (365). He never gave up this conception. In his later writings, he not only assumed a common mental nature, but he also supposed that the norm for language was its ability to effect the same state of mind toward things in separate persons. His example was of astronomers who, centuries apart, could use written symbols to obtain "the same adjustment to an external sequence as though it had occurred in a single man surviving throughout the interval." As a result, he could imagine that the emotion produced by a fine landscape would consist solely of sensations, immediate and remembered, and feelings remembered and inherited from "the race during barbarous times, when its pleasurable activities were chiefly among the woods and waters."[13] Spencer did not allow for the role of language in creating feelings.

Men still seek mathematical machine languages for scientific purposes, but they realize that any such system of linguistic levers gains speed, not force, of expression. Spencer's machine model for language calls for least "friction and inertia," whereas a model for literary language must account for a reader's sense of inexhaustible significance in a sentence (336). Human language bears a freight that is always inventoried unequally and incompletely by its speakers and readers. Being a medium of learning and socialization, every language is more powerful in subconscious and social significance than its user can fully grasp or control. The richness of language guarantees that it will never provide less than a double correspondence between speakers and between readers, not the single exchange that Spencer supposed. He was right to see the problem of literary expression as one of force, but wrong to suppose that its solution would be a reduction in heat loss. Inevitably, to do its work of getting acceptance—of lifting and sustaining interest—literary language must generate more significance than a reader can easily or ever realize.[14] So there must be a heat loss, for the sentence must perform work on the reader at the same time that it gives him light. A literary sentence need not be an efficient conveyance, but it must provide a powerful impetus. It need not glide, but it should seek force from a weight of significance propelled by natural sentence stresses.

Spencer, recommending a literary style that would send a reader flying toward sentence subjects, never allowed for the fact that the suggestivity of language was itself a thing of interest. Engineer and inventor, amateur of all sciences, always interested in physical things, Spencer never recognized that the variable meanings of writings were as worthy of sensuous and speculative apprehension as stars and rocks. So he could write, "Sad, indeed, is it to see how men occupy themselves with trivialities, and are indifferent to the grandest phenomena—care not to understand the architecture of the heavens, but are deeply interested in some contemptible controversy about the intrigues of Mary Queen of Scots!—are learnedly critical over a Greek ode, and pass by without a glance that grand epic written by the finger of God upon the strata of the Earth!"[15] Sad, too, that Spencer could not be fascinated by reasonings from historical documents (perhaps about Mary) or by interpretations of literary texts (like Pindar's odes).

Yet Spencer was sound in one aspect of his psychology of style. He knew that "the habitual mode of utterance must depend upon the habitual balance of nature. The predominant feelings have by use trained the intellect to represent them." Although this led him to speculate about the absolute artist—"a perfectly endowed man must unconsciously write in all styles"—he was aware of the relative stylist who must work to get any variety into his phrasing (366). He gave special attention in his essay to the arrangement of similes and metaphors. His own mature style reflects his predominant feeling of confidence, and most clearly so in its similes.

Toward the end of *The Study of Sociology*, Spencer offered a remarkable analogy for the slowness of progress.

> /1/ Light, falling upon a crystal, is capable of altering its molecular arrangements, but it can do this only by a repetition of impulses almost innumerable: *before a unit of ponderable matter can have its rhythmical movements so increased by successive etherial waves, as to be detached from its combination and arranged in another way,* millions of such etherial waves must successively make infinitesimal additions to its motion. /2/ *Similarly, before there arise in human nature and human institutions, changes having that permanence which makes them an acquired inheritance for the human race,* there must go innumerable recurrences of the thoughts, and feelings, and actions, conducive to such changes. /3/ The process cannot *be abridged;* and must *be gone* through with due patience.[16]

Here the two long *introductory sections* prepare the reader to accept the need for innumerable impulses before there can be permanent change. The *passive verbs* in sentence three suggest the appropriate patience with postponement of change in human institutions. The analogy perfectly expresses Spencer's confidence that the universe was Newtonian (and so required etherial waves), that acquired characters were inheritable, and that there were no other sources for lasting social changes than inheritable changes in individuals. But at the speed of light, the number of impulses per second becomes enormous: a crystal might well be changed. So in the twentieth century, hundreds of millions of human beings, whose most important inheritance is capacity for language and so for information and theory, can change their institutions in a generation exactly by innumerable recurrences of new sentences for their thoughts and feelings and actions. A hundred years after Spencer advised patience, people can communicate weighty sentences at the speed of light, and so they are not postponing lasting social changes.

CHAPTER 3

Metaphysics

AS widely read as *Education* (1861), *First Principles* (1862) suggested simple and vast conceptions and affirmed progress as inevitable.[1] It could appeal to opposite temperaments: Part I offered intimations of the mystical; Part II deduced an apparently scientific, magical formula for universal evolution. Even on reflection, the agnostic could agree with Part I and, like Huxley, worship at "the altar of the Unknown"; and a mechanist could find that Part II described all phenomena in terms of matter and motion.[2] The perorations of the two parts were reprises of pages honoring the wise man and the sincere man of science, that had concluded, respectively, *Social Statics* (1851) and "Progress: Its Law and Cause" (1857).[3] George Eliot, Beatrice Webb, and Arnold Bennett all admired the second eulogy, of the person who knew that absolute knowledge was beyond knowing, but who was no "timid sectarian . . . evincing the profoundest of all infidelity—the fear lest the truth be bad."[4] Intended as the first stage of Spencer's synthesis of science, *First Principles* proposed notions that remain curious enough to call for summarization.

I *Leading Ideas*

In Part I, Spencer relegated to indefiniteness all assertions of absolutes. He admitted the universality, independence, and vitality of religious sentiments; but he argued that both the theistic, and the atheistic, theories were inconceivable (28, 45 - 50). He quoted Henry L. Mansel's case that divine attributes of First Cause, Absolute, and Infinite were mutually contradictory. The Absolute would be one and simple, without relation to anything else; Cause, however, was a relation. If one said that the Absolute became the First Cause, then the Absolute had passed beyond former limits and so was not at first unlimited or Infinite. Spencer proposed that the absolute mystery about anything outside of experience should reconcile religion and science: "the Power which the Universe manifests to us is utterly inscrutable" (60)[5] Within experience, he pointed out the ultimate incomprehensibility of basic concepts—space, time, matter, force, and consciousness—unless they were related to unconditioned actualities (63 - 80).[6] To Spencer, the relative knowledge of conditioned, human life implied "a real Non-relative or Absolute." The limits of consciousness implied an abstract of those limits, indeed of all thoughts, an "ultimate mental element . . . necessarily indefinite and necessarily indestructible," which was conditioned in every thought and was the obverse of self-consciousness (107, 103 - 08). On this sense of something beyond thought, Spencer based his belief in objective reality. Having pointed out the limits of intelligence, he proposed a scientist's religion in these terms: submission to the limits of human intelligence (after denial of original sin); acceptance of all existence as existing through "The Unknowable"; toleration of perennial creeds and worship as vehicles of The Unknowable appropriate to their societies; and loyalty to one's own principles and sympathies. The last two attitudes he found necessary, since all beliefs were "elements in that great evolution of which the beginning and the end are beyond our knowledge or conception" (119, 123 - 24, 131 - 33).

The second and larger part of *First Principles* presented Spencer's philosophy of nature, which he called "transfigured realism" (175). He distinguished object from subject by the vividness of sensations relative to the faintness of other inner manifestations. Although he admitted that nothing could be conceived to be objectively real, he proposed that persistence of manifestations in consciousness was the ultimate test of the real for man, since all people have a notion of an absolute reality persisting under all forms (165 - 66). He found that ideas of matter, motion, space, and time, in that order, derived from "the ultimate datum of consciousness," the force of which one was conscious in his or her own muscular efforts. This force was the correlative of the unknowable, absolute reality (174 - 76).[7] He insisted that phenomena should not suggest illusiveness, since they recurred. Recurrent impressions together with one's persistent consciousness of something unlimited suggested that phenomena had real grounds or noumena (150, 166 - 67, 176). So Spencer pointed from phenomena to the inscrutable and felt that he had transfigured realism.

Matter and motion, derivatives of force, could no more disappear than their source. Force had to be persistent, since otherwise the unknowable cause of existence would be interrupted and existence discontinued. The Persistence of Force (or "the persistence of some Cause which transcends our knowledge") guaranteed the uniformity of law or the persistence of relations among forces (199). The chief law was the transformation and equivalence of forces—physical, chemical, psychological, sociological—of which a full explanation was no more possible than of the origin of force (223). Other laws were the direction of motion and matter always along the line of least resistance and, according to the resistances, along a characteristically undulating path. He exemplified his laws by illustrations from astronomy, geology, mechanics, biology, and from society. He argued that individuals in a society, for example, were impelled by their desires (forces) along lines of least resistance to them, and that each successive generation exhibited a wave of man's activity so that "Life . . . progressed . . . in immense undulations" (249, 266 - 68q).

Spencer devoted Part II of *First Principles* to describing laws and combining them into a comprehensive theory of change which he named "the law of evolution." He insisted that although any man's account of anything would always be incomplete, man's sphere of knowledge must include the entire perceptible history of each object, from inception to final disintegration (281 - 83). In such object-histories, Spencer noted the common antagonism in evolution, the integration of matter and dissipation of motion, and dissolution, the disintegration of matter through the absorption of motion (288). He recognized simple evolution, and compound evolution, in which motion was not immediately dissipated, but persisted through secondary redistributions of the object's parts.

Spencer aimed at showing that phenomena of all orders of existence might be ranged under his generalizations. Simple evolution was the integration of matter and the loss of applied motion. Some of Spencer's illustrations were chemical reactions induced by heat, early embryological stages, the prospect of a European federation, and losses of inflectional endings in English. Compound evolution involved the integration of parts of wholes and had three concurrent characteristics: heterogeneity, definiteness, and rhythm. Heterogeneity eventually resulted from the chain reactions of causes and effects initiated by every force that acted on masses of matter. Increasing definiteness accompanied greater heterogeneity by the segregation of like units of matter by incident forces (468). In other words, integration or primary redistribution made parts of wholes more definite, more distinctly marked off from each other. Secondary redistributions of parts made them more heterogeneous. Motion retained in parts also became more differentiated, while the motion of the whole became more definite. Spencer turned to what he called superorganic evolution—the results of the actions of associations of organic bodies—for many of his examples of compound evolution. By accepting current beliefs that European peoples were superior to savage peoples, he found illustrations of heterogeneity and definiteness in European physiques, languages, and arts and sciences. Examples of both heterogeneity of retained motion (from secondary redistributions of motion) and definiteness of retained motion (from primary redistribution of motion) were the variety of rhythms shown by the human digestive system and the circulation of the blood.

The complete formula was "Evolution is an integration of matter and concomitant dissipation of motion; during which the matter passes from an indefinite, incoherent homogeneity to a definite, coherent heterogeneity; and during which the retained motion undergoes a parallel transformation" (394). In all cases, there was "progress toward equilibration": the divergent forces rediverging and coming to balances in moving equilibria and finally ceasing in universal quiescence (479q., 508). Spencer's favorite example of equilibration was the spinning top. It first moves laterally, next oscillates or wobbles, then spins so uniformly on one spot that it appears stationary, and finally either wobbles into a fall or, if suspended, spins to a stop (480). He looked forward to the evolutionary limits of the individual in a perfect adjustment of mental force and all surrounding forces of the industrial society in an equilibrium of supply and demand (500, 503). Finally, Spencer found warrant—in the Persistence of Force—for belief in a "cosmical equilibration which brings Evolution under all its forms to a close . . . . only in [or rather, after] the establishment of the greatest perfection and the most complete happiness" (510 - 11).

In his second edition of *First Principles*, Spencer added, as further inferences from the Persistence of Force, not only the distinction between simple and compound evolution, but also his notion of dissolution. Since he had reasoned that motion, in reaching a limit, always produced the conditions for a counter movement, he rewrote his conclusions about cosmical Evolution to include a counter process of universal dissolution that must eventually follow evolution. Universal equilibration would be succeeeded by the gradual concentration of the solar system and the galaxy, collisions of stars, and dispersal of matter into nebulae (524 - 27). To Spencer's mind, this revision saved the phenomena of disintegration and made his theory as unified as possible: "one Evolution going on everywhere after the same manner" (537). By second thoughts, Spencer dispersed into indefinite process his first vision of universal perfection: ". . . if we are hence compelled to entertain the conception of Evolutions that have filled an immeasurable past and Evolutions that will fill an immeasurable future; we can no longer contemplate the visual creation as having a definite beginning or end, or as being isolated" (542).

II *Compelling Conceptions?*

Spencer suggested some of the definite beginnings of *First Principles,* but analyses have shown that his ideas were not conclusive. In 1849, Spencer had satisfied his uncle that although he believed that the ultimate nature of things was unknowable, he did not affirm atheism, but only that there must be some unknowable Cause of things.[8] At the end of "Progress" (1857), he professed "the unknowable": "inward and outward things" were "inscrutable in their ultimate genesis and nature."[9] In "The Nebular Hypothesis" (1858), he declared himself for an "Unknown Power," "a First Cause . . . transcending 'the mechanical God of Paley.' "[10]

By postulating the Unknowable, Spencer hoped to reconcile religion and science in a commonsense restraint from declarations about what could not be known. In the West, George Santayana accepted the Unknowable, but only as a knowable, animal faith in a real world.[11] Alexander Bain remarked that the Unknowable would be no bar to any metaphysician who wished to adopt theism.[12] In any case, Spencer's terms were imprecise. He referred to the Unknowable as either "a real Non-relative or Absolute" (108).[13] The first phrase is as unfit as the second for Spencer's purpose of defining the Relative: both phrases meet self-contradiction when related to anything.[14] The negation of the *in*conceivable may be inconceivable, not because there must be an Unknowable, as Spencer believed, but because the Relative is the only whole that need be postulated as knowable.[15] As Tolstoy's Levin felt, Spencer wrote Part I like "natural science writers who had never studied metaphysics."[16]

The novelty in Part I was Spencer's insistence on an unconditioned, indefinite consciousness. It was this mental element which existed absolutely that gave a sense of absolute existence (105, 107). In Part II, he explained that this consciousness derived from the absolute persistence in the mind of something surviving all changes of relation (166). In his psychology, Spencer spoke only of an underlying something, and appended an account of a form of consciousness in which "mind received a sensation passively without perceiving it."[17] At no time did he conceive of an Unconscious, and there was no scientific warrant for another term for the margin or "outskirts" of consciousness.[18] Rather, owing to his speculations in Part I, Spencer's philosophy became assimilable to the perennial philosophy, and especially to Taoism. The *Tao Teh Ching,* the central book of Taoism (c. 300 B. C., China) spoke of the Unnamable (the ineffable): "The Unnamable is of heaven and earth the beginning. The Namable becomes of the ten thousand things the mother. . . ." Spencer's Unknowable and knowable seemed analogous terms.[19]

Part II had its origin in Spencer's thinking and writing during the fifteen years after *Social Statics*. First fruits were the essays "Progress," "Transcendental Physiology," "The Nebular Hypothesis," and "The Classification of the Sciences." Thinking about organic, social, and inorganic development went on concurrently, but only after his partial recovery from his illness did Spencer's ideas mature one by one. In 1852, he had noted, in Carpenter's *Physiology,* Karl von Baer's law of embryological development from the homogeneous to the heterogeneous or special.[20] While writing his psychology in 1854, Spencer planned an essay that would apply von Baer's law to "all groups of phenomena."[21] In early 1857, he wrote "Progress: Its Law and Cause," in which he attributed heterogeneity to the multiplication of effects.[22] Writing the essay on physiology later that year, he reached the ideas of the instability of the homogeneous as the origin of evolution and of integration as a secondary process in evolution.[23] In "Progress," he had argued that the establishment of the nebular hypothesis would show that the universe "was once homogeneous" and had become heterogeneous.[24] In his 1858 essay on that theory, he followed Laplace in describing a nebular origin for the solar system. At this point he had sufficiently clarified his main ideas to enable him to explain continuity from nebula to life to man, without appealing to the First Cause of natural theology.[25]

While collecting his essays at the same time, he began to sketch a mechanics of evolution, including the correlation of physical forces, the principle of the conservation of physical force, "as it was then called," and views of motion as rhythmical and along a line of least resistance.[26] He planned then not only *First Principles*, but also its Parts III and IV on astronomic and geologic evolution, and volumes on biology, psychology, sociology, and ethics.[27] During the next two years, he refined his plan, finding his explanation of evolution in "the ceaseless re-distribution of matter and motion everywhere, and deciding to derive all physical principles" from the Persistence of Force.[28] He dropped Parts III and IV, saying organic evolution was "of more immediate importance"; but as he admitted later, his knowledge of higher mathematics, physics, and chemistry "was obviously inadequate."[29] His spring 1860 programme of the Synthetic Philosophy called for ten volumes, which would advance through parts called Data and Inductions to the leading aspects of each field of evolution.

All of the volumes were completed except the third on sociology, which was to have dealt with the development of language, science, and the fine arts.[30] While writing "The Classification of the Sciences" (1864), he noticed that integration was the primary process in evolution, and that differentiation was secondary.[31] So he proceeded to the second edition, still relying on organic and superorganic evolution for most of his illustrations of the Knowable, and still believing that progress was "not an accident, . . . but a beneficent necessity."[32] In the result, he let stand a variety of errors.

An elementary difficulty with Spencer's account of cosmic evolution was that it had a false beginning.The homogeneity that he supposed, a nebula, was in fact an enormous cloud of heterogeneous matter (402 - 06). Had it been homogeneous, it would have been stable, according to Newton's first law.[33] And in any case, the nebula from which the solar system concentrated was not the origin of the universe. In short, Spencer lacked precise scientific ideas as to origin.[34]

Spencer landed his accounts of matter and motion in a second difficulty by supposing the conceivable to be inconceivable. He argued that the annihilation of matter was unthinkable, since one could not perceive something disappear while it stood in its place. As the next chapter details, John Stuart Mill showed that one could imagine trying to see an object and not seeing it. But Spencer insisted on perceptions of the permanence of matter (182 - 83).

Similarly, he claimed that one could not conceive space relation separate from force and proceeded to exlain only the continuity (the average) of a pendulum's motion (191, 187 - 88). As students of physics knew, one needed to conceive of the acceleration of the pendulum in terms of its potential energy ("energy of position").[35] Spencer's distrust of "symbolic conceptions," led him to rely unnecessarily on picture-thinking from a "pre-Galilean age" of physics (41).[36]

Third, the affiliation of all evolutionary processes to the Persistence of Force amounted to a mystification, a sleight of hand, in detail and in method. Multiplication of effects, for example, was only a play on words for Persistence of Force (or Cause) in a chain of effects (199).[37] Yet the process came out as "the production of many changes by one cause," rather than what Persistence of Force called for: "equality of action and reaction," or many causes for many effects (437, 198).[38] Spencer's reminders about the "primordial truth" of Force amounted in fact, to "Abracadabra."[39] A chapter announced a principle, offered illustrations of it, and then declared that these illustrations not only established the principle "inductively," but also were "deducible from the deepest of all truths" (454).[40] Logically, the method of all of Part II amounted to a prolonged tautology, a sorites. Persistence of Force was the basis of physical concepts of matter and motion; these principles were the basis of evolution; the processes of evolution—instability of the homogeneous, multiplication of effects, segregation, and equilibration—were results of Persistence of Force; in short, one factor did all: Persistence of Force was Persistence of Force.[41] When Spencer argued, by appeal to Persistence of Force, that negation of the conservation of force was inconceivable, Mill "thought it out-Whewelled Whewell," the exponent of Supreme Cause and Fundamental Ideas.[42] James Clerk Maxwell was delighted with his friend Peter Tait's precise view of force, as an alternative to Spencer's Protean force, "Whose definitions, like a nose of wax, Suit each occasion."[43]

The terminology of *First Principles* was vague and ambiguous, and was inconsistently applied by Spencer. Maxwell explained to Spencer in 1873 not only that the motion of molecules was not rhythmical, but that "agitation" would be a better choice as one of the "words of little meaning," which scientists needed to use. Their words needed to express only what was proved by experiment, and should not connote any mere hypotheses.[44] Spencer's terms were vague and labelled several different results. "Coherent" meant cohesive, permanent, or mutually dependent; "integration" meant growth, embryonic differentiation, animal sociality, contraction, hardening, centralization, and generalization.[45] In a spoof of Spencer's formula, "differentiation" became "something-elseifications," and "integration," "sticktogetherations."[46]

Spencer spoke of his "formula" of evolution, but Tait insisted that it was only a definition, since it was not predictive.[47] It could not be so, since its phrases were not and could not be consistently related in one process. Part of the definition applied here or there, but the whole definition did not apply to the universe, as it should if it were to be a formula for universal evolution.[48] Sometimes integration of matter and dissipation of motion were concomitant. But living (integrated) things retained motion, and there was no integration of matter when animal sociality evolved. Neither result occurred when mental forces arose.[49] Spencer saw differentiation and segregation as concurrent processes; he did not see that they could be opposing or alternative ones, since one led to complexity (heterogeneity), and the other, to simplicity (definiteness).[50] Organic evolution showed progressive equilibration, but inorganic evolution did not. Rather, it showed local dissolution and, in general, diminishing heterogeneity, as the amount of energy *un*available for work increased. Even increase in biological organization coverted motion (energy) into heat which radiated into space. From there, even the Persistence of Force could not reconvert it as force for evolutionary work.[51]

As the next chapter will show, Spencer made brave efforts in *The Principles of Psychology* to overcome the dichotomy of mind and body. But as William James said, he could not keep a "mechanical point of view . . . for five pages consecutively"[52] For that reason he did not understand the second law of thermodynamics and its prediction of universal entropy. He was "staggered" when Tyndall told him in 1858 that universal equilibrium would mean death.[53] But he went on to forecast impossible cycles of evolutions and dissolutions.[54] The universe was not like one nebula; neither was its course open to deduction from the mathematical limits of finite space, time, and number, without knowledge of thermodynamics.[55] But Spencer imagined that the radiation of the stars would not be lost. It followed from the persistence of force that "the quantity of molecular motion given out" during all the integrations of Evolution would eventually reduce the galaxy to nebular form again

(527). An enormous number of Maxwell's demons, sorting molecules by their velocities, would have been necessary to reverse the levelling of molecular velocities—the heat loss—that Spencer ignored.

In his last, sixth edition, Spencer tried to reduce his claim of providing "*completely-unified* knowledge" in a philosophy of evolution (140).[56] But he retained his view that intuition of the Persistence of Force had priority to and higher warrant than investigations which led to quantitative evidence of the conservation of energy. Because of this unnecessary belief, Spencer thought that he could follow his own test of truth about "the totality of things" (542, 228).[57] So by 1874 some scientists felt that *First Principles* was an obstruction to experimental science, since its influential author would not think in symbols that did not refer to force. But one part of the definition of evolution—heterogeneity—had a truistic quality; and a century later scientists and social scientists continued to recognize evolution as development of complexity.[58]

Spencer's metaphysics were impressive to contemporaries who wanted natural science to be a vision in which "every single object suggests a vast sum of conditions."[59] When he offered a definition for cosmic evolution that promised progressive harmony in the universe, Spencer appeared to many to bind the smallest things with the greatest in a natural law.[60] Today it would be wrong to scorn a thinker whose universal process of equilibration can be recognized anew in theories that predict behavior to be a function of reinforcing environmental conditions.[61]

CHAPTER 4

Philosophy of Mind

THE principle of continuity began as the glory, but finally became the logical circle, in Spencer's philosophy of mind. In *The Principles of Psychology* he aimed at showing that body and mind could be viewed as counterparts, rather than opposites. The development of the central nervous system could be argued to have occurred by minute stages, and advance in intelligence could be regarded as correlative with advance in nervous organization. By this psychophysical parallelism, Spencer bravely attempted to overcome philosophical dualism. His correlations were admirable insofar as he kept clear that he was paralleling discontinuous series of phenomena each of which had its own order. He courted circular reasoning by his thoroughness in extending the principle of continuity from biology to psychology. From proposing that conception was only relatively different from perception, he went on to affirm uniformities in thoughts and things, which revealed much about his preference for certainty, but proved nothing. Similarly, trying to explain constancy in a person's perceptions, he suggested that the person had inherited functionally-produced modifications of the nervous system. But that required that feelings be transformable into physical forces capable of exercising nerves; and so, as in *First Principles*, all phenomena collapsed into Persistence of Force. Yet Spencer's effort to relate the individual's learning to the experiences of the species was innovative and plausible.

Spencer began writing *The Principles of Psychology* in 1854 from his "'fundamental conception" that mind should not be studied in isolation.[1] The development of intelligence could be inferred from the evolution of life: that is, from the adjustments of internal, physiological environments to external environments. The parallelism of physiological and psychological phenomena would be revealed by the correspondences of organisms to their environments. As from organism to organism nervous systems showed imperceptible gradations, so "the complication" of mind also arose by "insensible steps."[2] Since objects could only affect an organism through contact through skin and muscles, the tactual sense would become "the mother tongue" of impressions gained through eyes, ears, and nose. "A highly-elaborated tactual apparatus" would always accompany superior intelligence (P, I, 358q., II, 236). In this way, Spencer discarded as "but superficially true" his first view of the mind according to faculty psychology: mind as the seat of separate powers whose activities variously produced all sensations, memories, emotions, and thoughts.[3]

It was only a step for Spencer to base the association of impressions on the development of the nervous system of a species. Not instincts or innate ideas, nor the experience of the individual, would explain why an animal's or a person's perceptions were more or less constant (P, I, 470). The transcendentalists (e.g., Kant) claimed too much, while the empiricists (e.g., Mill) explained too little (P, I, 467). Rather, just as "new habits of life" bequeathed a "modified bodily structure," so they handed down "modified nervous tendencies" organized in the nervous system (P, I, 422). Experience did determine "all psychical relations whatever, from the necessary to the fortuitous," but many intuitions as well as reflexes and instincts, were inherited with a complex nervous system. The interactions of the ancestors of an animal with their environments pre-determined whether it was as educable as a man. A person's capability of knowing combinations of impressions derived from the human brain, which was "an organized register of infinitely-numerous experiences received" by the nervous systems of an enormous series of human and animal ancestors (P, I, 424, 470). Thus, by supposing the inheritance of functionally-produced modifications of the nervous system, Spencer extended the basis of associational psychology to the experiences of the "racial animal," and introduced "evolutionary associationism."[4]

While this approach, together with psychophysical parallelism, "greatly benefited the early stages of the study of psychology as a biological science," Spencer was unwise to extend the principle of continuity to reasoning. He elaborated a theory of knowledge that conflated perception and conception and reduced everything to Persistence of Force. It seems fatefully ironic that Spencer's ill health began when he was in the middle of his first chapter on reason. When he was arguing for use-inheritance and was ready to avow his adherence to the development hypothesis (P, I, 465-66n.), his usually graceful handwriting became cramped, angular, feeble, and irregular. Halfway into the next chapter, on feelings, he noted his poor health.[5]

When Spencer had begun his book, he had written his father that it would "ultimately stand beside Newton's *Principia*."[6] But Huxley was not persuaded, although he recognized Spencer as the only person he knew between 1851-58 who "compelled respect" and was "a thorough-going evolutionist."[7] Darwin did not notice Spencer's contribution to an evolutionary understanding of mind and brain until 1872.[8] Twenty years later, Tyndall claimed that Spencer's belief "was my belief also" in 1855, but then only Lewes and Mill were appreciative.[9] On rereading the book in 1864, Mill wrote Spencer praise for his affiliating mind and nerves, and so "removing the chief difficulty in the association psychology."[10] It is small wonder, then, that by 1867 Spencer felt he "had got all the kicks and others the halfpence," and would wish to bring out a second edition to establish his priority, which a recent writer had ignored.[11]

But *The Principles of Psychology* never caused the "sensation" for which Spencer had hoped in 1852.[12] Even the second edition was "cod-liver oil to the general," and he was resigned by 1877 that most people would prefer vile medicine to "a chapter of that book."[13] Indelible is one picture he recalled of his writing outdoors in Wales the crucial chapters on reason and the feelings: "I raised my head and saw, a few feet off in front, a semi-circle of sheep intently gazing at me: doubtless puzzled by a behavior unparalleled in their experience."[14] Most of Spencer's audience may have been puzzled, but the second edition became William James's textbook for his first class of undergraduates in psychology.[15] The leading idea of that edition, psychophysical parallelism, influenced the basic assumptions of Freud and of a leading British neurologist, John Hughlings Jackson (1835-1911), and Spencer's "deductive syntheses stimulated" Pavlov.[16]

I *Volume I (1870)*

Both the principle of continuity and evolutionary associationism reappeared in the second edition, since Parts III and IV were largely unchanged from 1855. Physiology, which dealt with many simultaneous vital processes, and psychology did not differ absolutely, since psychical phenomena only tended to be exclusively successive or serial (P, I, 395 - 96). The "thread of consciousness" had simultaneously "outer strands of changes" that were "indefinite and loosely adherent" and an "internal closely-twisted series of changes" (P, I, 405 - 406). The tendency for states of consciousness to follow each other varied with the persistence of relations in the environment as absolute, probable, or fortuitous, or in other words, with the frequency of experience of the relations (P, I, 408, 416 - 17, 460). Reflexes were simple, and instincts were compound, automatic coordinations predetermined by absolute or probable persistences. Memory began when psychical states were too involved to be automatic, and memory ceased when through repetition a succession became automatic (P, I, 450). There was a transition from instinct to reason so gradual that it was impossible to infer when the "correspondence . . . between inner and outer relations" had become too "complex, or special, or abstract, or infrequent" to be instinctive (P, I, 453 - 54). There was no "absolute distinction," therefore, "between animal intelligence and human intelligence" (P, I, 460).

Spencer argued that advance in intelligence was not only gradual, but also very slow. The effects of the most regular and recurrent experiences of relations in the environment were "bequeathed, principal and interest," and "slowly amounted to that high intelligence which lies latent in the brain of the infant" (P, I, 471). Many relations that were more or less constant became "congenitally represented by more or less complete nervous connexions" (P, I, 470). Later, Spencer declared that all "mental phenomena . . . of any considerable complexity" were "results of the inheritance of functionally-produced modifications."[17] In Volume II, he noted that the rapidity with which sensations succeeded each other must have been established imperceptibly in the nervous system by prolonged habit. The process would have been physiological and, consequently, "extremely slow" (P, II, 296).

Spencer also speculated that emotions were innate coordinations of elementary feelings. Love, for example, was "the most compound" and so "the most powerful, of all the feelings"; yet it occurred in a person before he could learn it (P, I, 487q., 488, 494). Emotions became established in the innate nervous structure by habitual experience of complex sets of circumstances that had a general likeness. Corresponding to probable, rather than to absolute external relations, emotions would not be uniform in composition, but every manifestation of an emotion would have a family resemblance. Like sunsets painted on glass and superimposed on each other, experiences of an emotion would show a general, massive pattern, but their details would be vague (P, I, 491 - 93). Spencer developed his analysis of emotions at the end of the second edition as a bridge to his ethics and sociology.

In Volume I there appeared three new parts in support of the theory that simultaneous neural and mental events were counterparts. Spencer had written a short essay on "The Physiology of Laughter" in 1860, and must have been pleased to see Darwin cite it and Part V of Volume I in *The Expression of the Emotions in Man and Animals* (1872).[18] The central nervous system consisted of organs for levels of coordination, marked in Spencer's usual terminology as simple (spinal cord), compound (medulla oblongata), and doubly-compound in space (cerebellum) and in time (cerebrum) (P, I, 61, 555 - 56). He also took notice of the unconscious actions of the visceral and vaso-motor nerves, saying later that mind is "as deep as the viscera" (P, I, 104).[19]

In Part I, he acknowledged that there was no proof that feeling and neural occurrence were "the inner and outer faces of the same change" (P, I, 128). But he pointed to numerous congruences, such as the direct proportion in intensities of feelings and of correlative neural events. He pointed out that the unit of the intermittent "nerve-current" was a "pulse of molecular action" and that the "ultimate unit of consciousness" was "a nervous shock." The last term was misleading, since it implied more for his theory than its denotation, which was only "strong pulse of subjective change," "mental shock," or "pulse of feeling" (P, I, 151 - 53). William James objected to such "scandalous vagueness" in terminology.[20] Spencer, however, might feel innocent, since he had conceded that it would be illogical to identify a unit of motion, "the oscillation of a molecule," with the unit of feeling, a nervous shock (P, I, 158). Because the nervous system could greatly amplify impulses both in sensory and in motor nerves, there existed quantitative correlation of feeling and molecular motion only in the nerve center where the feeling arose (P, I, 118, 120).[21]

The new parts of Volume I added many such clarifications and correlations that gave impressive support to Spencer's psychology. From "Progress: Its Law and Cause" (1857) came the observation that introspection revealed not consciousness, but only an already past state of it. Mind was distinct from what it contemplated: "the substance of Mind escapes into some new form in recognizing some form under which it has just existed" (P, I, 147).[22] Introspection could discover two classes of feelings: homogeneous states of consciousness (feelings proper) and momentary feelings at the transition from one state to another. The latter, relational feelings were nervous shocks, the units of composition of states of mind (P, I, 164).[23] Introspection could also distinguish sensations, started at the periphery of the nervous system, and emotions, initiated at the center (P, I, 167). This horizontal classification by structure went along with a vertical one by function: sensations from the surface or interior of the body were relatively vivid; central or ideal feelings were relatively faint. But emotions, and especially desires, could be vivid. After reviewing Alexander Bain's work in 1860, Spencer developed a four-step classification of both feelings and relations of feelings from vivid to ideal: presentative (any sensation or localizing of a sensation), presentative-representative (any emotion or perception), representative (any recollected sensation or emotion; any memory), re-representative (any sentiment or abstraction) (P, II, 513 - 14).[24]

Introspection discovered no permanence in states of consciousness. Psychical changes were not independent of physical changes, as "parallelism" might suggest, but were their "obverse" (P, I, 508).[25] Recurrence of either vivid, or faint feelings implied persistence in non-mental agencies—in both the nervous system and in objects external to it (P, II, 463 - 64, 481 - 82, 485 - 86). Spencer worked out interesting "objective correlatives," therefore, for the two kinds of feelings (P, I, 270). Relational feelings were very brief, since they corresponded to the rapid transmission of molecular waves through a nerve fiber. A feeling, on the other hand, had duration, since it corresponded to a continued transformation of a nerve center by the waves brought by a nerve fiber (P, I, 190). When a disturbance at the ends of a nerve reverberated through the central nervous system, there could be consciousness of a vivid feeling (P, I, 125 - 27). And if there had been pre-experiences of the sensation, similar but faint feelings could become the concomitants of the molecular motions in the higher, compound centers of coordination (P, I, 96, 105). An idea resulted when a vivid feeling associated in this way with one or more like, faint feelings (P, I, 182). The associability of like feelings answered to the localization in the nervous system of correlative neural events (P, I, 257 - 58). The revivability and cohesion of feelings depended on their vividness and frequency (P, I, 233, 250 - 51). Similarly, according to the strength and the repetition of waves of motion through a nerve along "a line of least resistance," a symmetrical arrangement of a series of molecules was set up that could pass on more and more discharge to a nerve center (P, I, 511 - 19, 578). Finally, Spencer decided that phrenologists had been right to localize functions in the cerebrum, but wrong to mark precise regions in what was preeminently the center of coordination (P, I, 574 - 75).

II *Mind as Machine*

There is one great problem with Volume I: the passivity of mind as Spencer saw it.[26] He compared the nervous system to an elaborate player-piano: afferent nerve endings being the keys; medulla oblongata, the steel wires; and cerebellum and cerebrum, "vast magazines of [attached] tune-boards." When the pianist played some bars, he set going the attached apparatus, and it gave out concerts of melodies in faint tones. So, when the medulla oblongata was "played upon through the senses by external objects," the cerebrum and cerebellum played back faint feelings (P, I, 566 - 68). The piano and its appliances were permanent. The notes would die away as other ones were sounded in the apparatus, just as feelings faded when correlative waves of molecular motion ceased in the nervous system (P, II, 484 - 85). If higher nervous centers played on lower ones and aroused emotions, great combinations of ideal feelings, the sound arising in the piano would be "echoes of all kindred chords and cadences" that had been struck in the apparatus—the nervous system—during an immemorial past. Without its added appliances, the piano could still be played upon, and without the cerebellum and cerebrum the medulla oblongata would still coordinate vital processes (P, I, 571 - 72n.).

So Spencer granted no power of initiative to brain or mind. The power for piano or brain came from outside it, and the structure simply transformed it (P, I, 622). Impetus was received from "certain forces which pervade the Universe" (P, II, 144) These were few, since the great number of external phenomena were static or passive. Consciousness, nevertheless, was always changing and could represent "no-change" only by a duplication of an immediately previous state of mind (P, II, 277 - 78). It seems strange that Spencer could be satisfied with his illustration of mind as an elaborate perpetual motion machine. But his assumption that states of motion were facts of nature, rather than being subject to human influence, was normal before relativity theory invited man to accelerate matter to the speed of light.[27] He respected the "constructive imagination"; but given the physics of his time and his view of language, he could not conceive how mind could be initiatory (P, II, 535, 537).

Today it appears that brain synapses activate more at random than according to a line of least resistance.[28] Conditioned reflexes can be established rapidly and can take the place of others if need be. Instincts are not simply compound reflex actions, since they show a purposiveness that may end in a reflex response to one sensory stimulus.[29] Real as the physical environment, there is for man a social environment in which the connection of inner and external nexuses is some language.[30] Human intelligence, then, is meanings. Pavlov followed Spencer in recognizing in animals and humans the signalization of "a few unconditioned external agents" by "inborn" reflexes and by "a unified signalising system" of "conditioned connexions" and associations. But Pavlov also recognized in humans "another system of signalisation"—speech—whereby the signals of the first system were generalized, analyzed, synthesized, and thereby regulated.[31]

Language is a biologically founded, but culturally learned medium for coordinating feelings and social activity.[32] Because the grammar of any language allows people to produce an infinite number of sentences, language is the prime source for people's initiation and sharing of choices for action. A hundred years after Spencer's psychology, it is clear that minds are not separate pianos, but pianists with and for others. Because they are speakers and readers of secondary signalling systems, people can play and compose piano duets and can also move and build pianos. Through communication and cooperation, people practice choice; with each other in mind, they generate and select their options from the infinite possibilities of one language or another. This is the fourth dimension available to human consciousness. It is ironical that Spencer wrote as if he and all people were shut out of it. He did so, since he viewed language as having almost totally lost its original, clear mimicry of things and become a hindrance to thought.[33] Beginning with inferences of likeness, languages had developed from naming, the direct imitation of things, into apparatuses of symbols that interfered with thinking. Such half-truths could not seem more wrong today.

III *Volume II (1872): A Necessity for Certainties*

In seeking to explain the genesis of men's conceptions, Spencer's conception of language made it easy for him to neglect all systems of symbols, whether those of mathematics, logic, or language. He could proceed according to the principle of continuity to distinguish reasoning (or conception) from perception only relatively. Though it was an indirect inference of relation between two things, reasoning tended to become more direct like perception, and so the transition was insensible (P, II, 134 - 35). Both perception and conception were "ideas" and involved representation from sensations. A concept had to be "figured in thought" by at least "symbols idealized from our sensations."[34] One could, on the other hand, "shut out all words and all the speculations conveyed through words, and . . . conception of the object [would] remain as vivid as ever" (P, II, 441). Language imitated "the [one] fundamental relation of subject and object" [rather than expressing a culture's view of that relation[35]], and otherwise would be "impotent as an amputated limb in empty space" (P, II, 335). Logic was based on intuitions that had been acquired by inheritance, and was an objective science, since it represented connections of external objects which existed "in some form" (P, II, 87). In short, formal considerations were insignificant to Spencer. He forgot that he had quoted with approval the example of Laplace, who had "invented" "artifices" in mathematics.[36] He never recognized that language was another arbitrary, non-representative symbol system facilitating thought, and that the test of logical propositions was self-contradiction.

In "The Universal Postulate" (1853; Part I, 1855) and in Volume II, Spencer meant to overcome the inability of contemporary empiricists to assert a causal relation between subject and object.[37] Mill, like Bain, could not avoid solipsism, for he could only assert knowledge of his own states of mind.[38] Spencer proposed, as a test of objective truth, that one could not deny belief whenever a subject and a predicate were invariably united in thought. Supposing that predication was the "assertion that something *is*," he argued that "truths of immediate perception [had] the same warrant as the so-called necessary truths."[39] There was no better guarantee than "the intuition of sense," since logical necessity in propositions or mathematics was gained from experience.[40] He scorned any "mere game of symbols," for "answering to each absolute uniformity in nature which we can cognize, there must exist in us a belief of which the negation is inconceivable, and which is absolutely true."[41] This belief that "absolute uniformities of Thought correspond to absolute uniformities of Things" led Spencer through a long circle of argument (P, II, 426). The first point to notice, however, is the one which Mill never could make Spencer understand. He never saw that his warrant of sameness meant that he was treating perception and conception, and so the empirical and logical modes of speech, as alike.[42]

The friendly argument with Mill extended over a decade. Spencer's position was that when he was cold or when he was looking at the sun, he could not conceive that he was warm or that he was looking into darkness.[43] So long as he looked at the sun, the subject and predicate coexisted as invariably ('that is light') as they did in an axiom of logic. A perception was temporary, but otherwise it was as much a thought as a conception, as Spencer's use of "think" shows: "it is impossible to gaze at the sun and think it green, it is quite possible to gaze at the sun and think of a square (P, I, 245). Mill replied that invariability of belief was not equivalent to inconceivability.[44] He wrote Spencer, "I can, in broad daylight, *conceive myself* then and there looking into darkness." Mill could imagine "oneself trying to see and not seeing," and so could have a conception of darkness, even while looking at the sun. He suggested to his friend that there was a "transition from conception to belief—from an imagination of something thought as absent from the senses, to an apprehension of something which is thought to be present to the senses."[45]

Spencer had proposed an empirical test for propositions; Mill might explode it by denying it. A belief (a perception) could be tested empirically: what one is then and there looking into is a matter of fact. But the test of a conception was its logical necessity: the relation of the predicate to the subject must be analytic (a meaning of the subject) so that negation would result in contradiction. The test of Mill's conception would lie not in his imagining it, but in the form that he might give it.[46] Spencer did not see that his universal empirical postulate for both perceptions and propositions had been exploded. Had he done so, he would have had to question his application of the principle of continuity to mental processes (P, II, 134,). That would have been damaging to his entire psychology. At most he admitted only that sensation and perception, and emotion and cognition, tended to exclude each other from consciousness (P, II, 247, 438; I, 475 - 78). In his theory, he could not have recognized, as phenomenologists do, the exclusiveness of each intention of mind.

Because of his conflation of perception and conception, Spencer overestimated the significance of perception and underestimated the possibilities of conception. He called perceptions "thoughts" and denied or unduly restricted reasoning. In an 1865 essay on Mill and in Volume II, he contrasted the perception of food in one's mouth, as "the nascent *thought* of an independent existence," with the conception that one "cannot know what this is which lies outside of him." But then he denied "such self-criticism" as "a mere verbal conclusion to which his *thoughts* [would] not respond." He went on to assert that the perception was "consciousness of [the food] as a *reality*," rather than what would have been consistent, a vivid feeling related to other feelings arising from muscular tension (P, II, 452).[47] In another place, he held that perception of such feelings "disabled [one] from *conceiving*" *external* force except "as equivalent, both in quantity and *nature*" to muscular tension (P, II, 237). Yet in Volume I he had pointed out logical difficulties in translating units of external force into feeling (P, I, 160 - 61). There he had said that one could know only feelings, which were only symbols of something called "resistance," and that one could not even conceive the natures of actions outside himself (P, I, 206). In Volume II, he granted that the proposition was "*verbally* intelligible" that external force differed in nature from feelings of it. Then in the same sentence he disallowed that people could "*frame a conception* of force in the non-ego different from the conception we have of force in the ego (P, II, 239). This last conception was "a generalization of muscular sensations": a perception (P, II, 235).

Spencer's theory of knowledge suffered from his failure to recognize the functions of language as a system of symbols secondary to feelings. Without this insight, he could treat images from perceptions as if they were philosophical conceptions. There was force in consciousness; feeling was force; "active energy . . . well [ed] up from the depths of our consciousness"; and a cluster of vivid, or of faint feelings was "a fountain of power" (P. II, 479 - 83; I, 161). Since no word in Spencer's philosophy was more important than "force," his uncritical use of it was most damaging. Whereas Spencer, supposing that the notion of likeness to things underlay all language, could perceive "a psychical force known as effort," Mill and Huxley could conceive that "force" was, respectively, a "logical fiction," and " 'a name for the hypothetical cause of an observed order of facts' " (P, II, 124; I, 117).[48]

Spencer conceded to the Danish translator of his psychology that it was incomprehensible what "the force constituting consciousness" was and how a transformation of it could take place. But he insisted that "mental force" could "initiate a motor discharge."[49] The translator recognized Spencer's position that the evolution of the nervous system might be explained in terms of matter and motion, but he had reminded Spencer of his admission that the evolution of mind could not be so explained (P, I, 508; II, 485 - 86). Yet Spencer could only offer the analogy of consciousness to a piece of platinum wire in an electrical circuit of copper wires. As the current passing through the platinum was stronger, the platinum became more incandescent. But Spencer overlooked the facts that the platinum allowed the current to pass and 'initiated' no current, and that the light and heat generated in the platinum by the current were in no way transformed back into electricity. He revised, but never quite corrected the places cited by the translator from *First Principles*, where he had taught that "states of consciousness" were "modes of force," and that "mental forces" were transformations of "physical forces" and "retransformable" into "mechanical motion." While he was prepared to assert these changes as "mysteries," the translator declared that he could not find Spencer's account "quite clear."[50]

Some other second thoughts in the 1870's suggest that something deeper than the principle of continuity was at stake for Spencer in his perception of force. In 1876, P. G. Tait demonstrated that mathematically force was a vector, the rate of space variation of energy.[51] In 1880, Spencer granted that relations in space without reference to perceptions of muscular tension might be a sufficient mode of conceiving for physics. But it was inconceivable in philosophy, since ideas of muscular tension were the "ultimate symbols" into which all our other mental symbols were interpretable.[52] Yet after a mathematician objected to them, he omitted from *First Principles* two sentences expressing his perception of force: "Deeper than demonstration—deeper even than definite cognition—deep as the very nature of mind is the postulate at which we have arrived (i.e., the Persistence of Force). Its authority transcends all other whatever; for not only is it given in the constitution of our own consciousness, but it is impossible to imagine a consciousness so constituted as not to give it."[53] By removing these sentences, Spencer retreated from claiming the universal postulate, and simply presupposed Persistence of Force. He left it that he really meant "the persistence of some Cause" which transcended our knowledge and conception, and which one assumed in order to guarantee that action and reaction would be equal and opposite so that one could measure force.[54]

One reason for Spencer's reliance on his perception of consciousness as force was his distrust of formal patterns as merely verbal or as idealized symbols. He had, however, another reason. He wished to find in the "substance of mind" a "persistence" that could be the counterpart of the one that he had assumed in matter (P, I, 146). Although he said that Persistence of Force would have "the deepest assignable warrant," since it signified "an Unconditioned Reality, without beginning or end," actually persistence of "an underlying something" forming mind would be the warrant of this Cause (P, I, 226, 145).[55] So Spencer wrote of "active energy," and "fountains of power," welling up from "the depths" of consciousness. So he made *perception* of force the basis of all perceptions and conceptions of things. One must be "obliged to think" of force "as subjectively and objectively the same," to warrant belief in Persistence of Force. So one must be "obliged to symbolize" mechanical force or resistance as "the equivalent of muscular force": that is, as relations of feelings of muscular tension (P, II, 237).[56] If the negation of the perception of force were inconceivable, then causality could not be negated, Persistence of Force in external things would guarantee awareness of subject and object, and a world without a Supreme First Cause (God) would still show universal and inevitable laws.[57]

That Spencer wanted certainty of uniformity is evident from contradictory statements in his theory of "transfigured realism." In the chapter so titled (xix, Part VII), he said that objective phenomena could be represented by subjective effects "in such way that each change in the objective reality causes in the subjective state a change exactly answering to it—so answering as to constitute a cognition of it." Although the representation would be so distorted that its relations "would differ entirely" from the objective relations, it would register exactly any change in the latter and one could know it (P, II, 497). To reach this virtual impossibility, Spencer contradicted his declarations in Volume I about "an unknown something beyond consciousness" in which subjective relations, "as we know them, do not obtain" (P, I, 208, 233).[58] When the point was criticized, Spencer explained that he had meant "a relative cognition," like the correspondence between a balance sheet and money or goods.[59] The explanation showed that he desired certainty more than a consistent conception of hypothetical realism.

At the end of Volume I, Spencer forgot his many relativistic qualifications and asserted that "the order of [Ultimate Reality's] manifestations throughout all mental phenomena proves to be the same as the order of its manifestations throughout all material phenomena" (P, I, 627).[60] Yet he had already noted the tendency of states of consciousness to become serial. In Volume II, he disclosed that an order of two identical states of consciousness symbolized "outer statical phenomena," and he conceded that in general "the inner order of effects must be made to differ from the outer order of causes" (P, II, 277 - 78, 505*pp*). Transfigured realism became a "mighty boomerang" because Spencer was willing to say that his symbols—Mind, Feeling, Force, Matter, Motion—were, after all, like ultimate reality.[61] Then the underlying something and the Cause were not "inscrutable" (P, I, 162). Spencer's elaborate marching up and down again between interfaces—underlying Mind::consciousness; sensations::nerve centers; nerve ends::external forces; Matter::Persistence of Force (Cause)—seemed to have been for naught. He would have been safe had he only postulated an objective nexus, for his transfigured realism could not yield any knowledge of an object beyond consciousness.[62] He might claim that invariable beliefs were evidence of uniformities in nature, but that only led him in a circle that now must be traced.

In 1853 he had said that conceptions of Space, Time, Motion, Matter, and Force were beliefs founded on instinct.[63] In 1855, and again in 1870, he had argued that the inheritance of nervous connections founded in ancestral experiences, enabled those conceptions (and many other relations) to be intuitions. In 1872, he argued that the inconceivability of the negation of a mathematical axiom resulted from the fixity of correlative nervous structures caused by "habit in thousands ["nay, probably millions"] of generations" (P, II, 419, 505z). From there it was only a step for Spencer to assert that laws of the universe, like Newton's laws of motion, were "mental forms generated by ancestral experiences."[64] "Intuitions . . . latent in the inherited brain" made "the simplest uniformities of nature . . . better known than they are as experienced during an individual life."[65] But if in this way some cognitions became, as Spencer was fond of saying, *a priori* (self-evident) from having been *a posteriori* (derived from experience), the laws of the universe might also become necessities of thought (P, II, 195, 414). Then everything would prove everything; nothing could be a fact, for nothing would be falsifiable.[66]

This was the universe toward which Spencer's philosophy was

moving. He recalled that as a boy he had known "by intuition the necessity of equivalence between cause and effect."[67] In Parts III and V of his psychology, he pointed to the correspondence of outer and inner (neurological) actions, and deduced the development of the central nervous system from the Persistence of Force (Cause) between environment and mind. But then in Parts IV, VI, and VII, he assumed a "causal relation" between environment and development both of nervous structures, and of relations of feelings.[68] The inheritance of functionally-produced modifications assumed that mental force as well as external force exercised nervous structures (P, II, 419).[69] So Spencer was deducing the development of mind itself from the Persistence of Force, which he had denied to be a logically possible procedure (P, I, 508, 160 - 61).[70]

Accepting Spencer's hypothesis as to inheritance, one could say that the laws of nature must be "prefigurations of the forms of [the] intellect."[71] Spencer never said as much, but his procedure was to establish the congruity of fundamental intuitions with all other data of consciousness. Complete congruity would be "the complete unification of knowledge in which Philosophy [would reach] its goal" (P, I, 128).[72] By his tautological device, inheritance of acquired characteristics, the continuity of development would be universal in inorganic and organic existence, and would inevitably bring about the complete congruity of *a priori* knowledge and the laws of nature. Then all would be just as it must be. All laws of nature would be invariable beliefs, and all would be right with the world.

As a result of his theory of knowledge, Spencer limited his own conceptualizing. He became very conservative about hypotheses, seeing them as "incipient inductions" from perceptions (P, II, 84).[73] A controversy during the spring of 1874, when he was a candidate for the Royal Society, showed Spencer's inflexibility. A critic had quoted against him Professor Tait's (textbook) position that Newton's three laws "must be considered as resting on convictions drawn from observation and experiment and not on intuitive perception."[74] Spencer cited Professor Tait's remark that "the properties of matter might have been such as to render a totally different set of laws axiomatic," asked how Tait knew about things that were not, and invited him to report his experiments.[75] Tait's reply was a tale of a University student of algebra who stymied himself by wondering, "But what if *X* should turn out, after all, *not* to be the unknown quantity."[76] Spencer remarked that no one could see the point of the story.[77] Tait said that Spencer was the only man in England who failed to see the point of it. Like the student, Spencer could not abide the uncertainty of saying, "Let X be the unknown." Things as they are could not be open to speculation; about them men must have intuitive perceptions. Conception could not be a game of symbols to be refereed by observation and experiment; symbols must represent perceptions or they could not be "figured in thought" (P, II, 409n.).[78] Spencer could only apply the story to Tait, who had imagined an unknown set of laws.

Spencer could not see how his views that natural laws could be inherited intuitions, and that there was one empirical test for perception and conception, inhibited him from conceiving possibilities contrary to perception. It was impossible for him to see the distinction between what was logically inconceivable and what was only unimaginable according to accepted concepts.[79] Darwin counselled that a scientist's "reason should conquer his imagination."[80] Alternatively, one could say that Spencer's inflexibility about conception led him to deny Imagination to the scientist. He allowed only one empirical logic of classification, one geometry, one physics, and one evolution. He could not conceive of a universe without three dimensions and the ether, or an evolution without inheritance of acquired characteristics (P, II, 284, 505*kk*).[81] He could not have followed contemporary physics into fields of force, or have appreciated E. A. Abbott's *Flatland*, or have failed to attack Weismann's germ-plasm theory of inheritance.

Yet Spencer possessed a strong constructive imagination. He was ingenious at both psychophysical parallelism and at associational psychology—at correlating the conscious moves of the mind with the unconscious actions of the nerves, and at extending learning by association from the individual's experience to the experiences of the species. On the first score, he aimed at transcending the dualism of body and mind by his regard for touch, sensations of resistance, as the native language of thought. Touch was the register of one's first sensations and the interpreter of all other sensations. That he did not cite precursors like Hartley and Berkeley and that his logic was circular ought not to cancel one's respect for his attempt to overcome dualism.[82] His second attempt was to provide, in evolutionary associationism, a uniform natural law for human progress. That his philosophy of mind rested use-inheritance on a tautology should not prevent one from appreciating the imaginative plausibility of Spencer's case.

In his own day, his strength of mind soothed George Eliot, who reread *The Principles of Psychology* for "emotional relaxation" after she had finished writing *Adam Bede* (1859).[83] In 1872 and 1874, physiologist W. B. Carpenter and physicist John Tyndall recommended Spencer's transfigured realism in their Presidential Addresses to the British Association.[84] It is perhaps only a little sad to see Spencer observe in his last years that despite his proof of "the objective nature of logic, . . . the old idea persists without even a sign of change."[85]

CHAPTER 5

Ethics

SPENCER published *The Data of Ethics* in 1879, twelve years before *The Principles of Ethics,* since he felt that "the gap left by [the] disappearance of the code of supernatural ethics" had to be filled by "a code of natural ethics."[1] He intended his twenty-five years' work on his philosophy of evolution to be "a basis for a right rule of life, individual and social."[2] His friend Youmans said that he "jumped over to ethics" to answer those who were wondering whether evolution had anything to do with morality.[3] By 1893, Spencer had provided "a corrected and elaborated version" of the absolute ethics of *Social Statics,* where he had supposed that people had an innate moral sense, which was guiding them toward the realization of the Divine Idea, man's happiness (E, I, v). The correction was a theory of the development of moral intuitions, and the elaboration, a set of examples of least wrong conduct in given social conditions. The result was, as Huxley said, an account of the evolution of ethics and not a developed ethics.[4]

I *The Ideal Goal—The Evolution of Absolute Ethics*

The Principles of Ethics made Spencer's optimism especially evident. Elsewhere he held that universal evolution would be followed by universal dissolution, and that evolution was not inevitable in every society.[5] In his ethics, he insisted not only that adaptation to social conditions would increase, but that "progress" could not cease until "the highest social life" was reached. Although he blithely forecast that eventually pleasure would "accompany every mode of action demanded by social conditions," he granted that his arguments in the work were "valid only for optimists" (E, I, 185-86; II, 465). Had he not identified evolution with progress, he could have considered arguments as to why people should not allow evolution in another direction than the one he proposed.

Instead, since mankind was changing, he declared (as he had in

Social Statics) that absolute ethics were necessary for men's guidance toward one ideal goal (E, I, 275).[6] The perfect conduct of the ultimate man, i.e., producing pure pleasure, would be the fulfillment of Absolute Ethics (E, I, 261, 183). Such conduct would slowly evolve from the inheritance of the effects of pleasurable and painful experiences. It was by this view—that happiness was the ultimate, not the immediate end—that Spencer always distinguished his ethics from the utilitarian ethics of Bentham and the Mills. Spencer subscribed to the hedonistic view that an act was right if one gained from it more pleasure than pain. But as he had in *Social Statics*, he objected to the utilitarian aim of calculating from one's acts the greatest pleasure for the greatest number, since people could never know enough to calculate the consequences of their acts. He protested to John Stuart Mill that he was not thereby anti-utilitarian; but he certainly was a reverse utilitarian, since he opposed the "direct estimation" of pleasures and pains and reinstated moral intuitions *via* evolution.[7] The assertion that people could intuit what they ought to do had always been anathema to the utilitarians, but Spencer explained to Mill that he aimed to identify "moral intuitions" from which he could deduce the "laws of conduct" leading to the happiness of the greatest number.[8]

Consequently, one change from *Social Statics* was the substitution of the "accumulated effects of inherited experiences" for an unchanging innate (inborn) moral sense (S, 84; E, I, 470 - 71).[9] Similarly, the faculty of sympathy, an innate faculty in *Social Statics* (with credit given to Adam Smith), became a range of instinctive feelings produced by "experiences of pleasurable or painful results" (S, 89; P, II, 619q., 620, 576).[10] The instinct of personal rights, which led people to claim exercise of their capabilities as their natural right, became the egoistic sentiment of liberty, and then the ethical intuition of justice. Along with the sentiment of justice developed the other altruistic sentiments of self-restraint and generosity. Of these moral emotions, only that of liberty or equal freedom could have already become "an *a priori* belief" founded on "the experiences of innumerable successive individuals" (E, II, 56q.; P, I, 490). This belief remained, as in *Social Statics*, the view that each person had freedom to do his or her will, providing that another's freedom was not infringed. Only when war ceased to be a form of the struggle for existence could liberty and the other highest moral emotions develop fully (P, II, 577; E, I, 245, 293, 297). Ultimately, justice, both egoistic and altruistic, would become the necessary condition, and the two beneficent sentiments, the sufficient condition for the greatest happiness of all.[11]

By this strategy, Spencer believed that he had reconciled the utilitarians with the intuitionists, who claimed that all people were born with a power whereby they could know virtue.[12] He said that he had "harmonized" the "expediency-theory of morals with the intuitional theory" in what he called "rational utilitarianism" (E, II, 42 - 43; I, 162). But since he specified that the belief in equal freedom had developed in "part of the human race only," his absolute ethics could not be satisfactory to the intuitionists. And since he asked the utilitarians to give up their calculus of the pleasures of equal men and their reliance on individual experience, it was unlikely that they would resolve to wait on evolution for pure pleasure in a distant future. Indeed, in his own terms, "absolute" and "evolution" were in contradiction, unless the former was understood only as "highest."[13]

II *Practice—Ethics during Evolution*

While people were not fully adapted to the requirements of social life, they would experience pain, and their best conduct would be the least wrong (E, I, 186, 261). They could trust, as evolved adaptations, that physical pleasures would be correlatives of beneficial actions; but emotional pleasures and pains would still be maladjusted to social life (E, I, 79, 87; P, I, 279 - 80). Their ancestors having been first isolated brutes, then pre-social nomads, and afterwards social beings who found inflicting pain pleasurable, their simple, "earlier-evolved" feelings would still be much determined by anti-social ancestral experiences. Therefore, they could only hope to adjust to social life by giving up immediate impulses and selecting "later-evolved" feelings that aimed at remote results (E, I, 114, 112).[14] This had been "the essence of the moral life" for Spencer since *Social Statics*, where he had insisted on the postponement of gratification (S, 74, 290).[15] So he assumed, for example, that the habit of repressing facial expressions, bodily movements, and speech intonations was caused by need to conceal feelings that would produce discord or estrangement (E, I, 247 - 48). From a man who claimed that he never swore until he was thirty-six, this claim of a need for abstinence from emotional pleasure is either exaggeration or priggishness.[16]

The remote results that would be least wrong for an individual to seek would be "the greatest length, breadth, and completeness of life" possible with a given inherited nature and the current national character (E, II, 3q.; I, 551). "The relatively more evolved conduct" increased life by being self-preserving, by gaining just benefits, or by advancing sympathies (E, I, 25). The first two results were essential, for the survival of the fittest in social terms depended on everyone's accepting the consequences of his conduct and nature (E, II, 60).[17] The sympathies, on the other hand, could not increase life as long as they involved much more emotional pain than pleasure (E, I, 246). One would be least wrong if he restrained himself from gaining the last benefit from competition and if he were generous when it not only lessened another's pain but promised remote results to the individual and society. (E, II, 277, 430). Strong sympathies would be a curse, however, were they not continually repressed when others' misery was "irremediable." Spencer was aware of the sufferings of masses of people in the British Isles: he named the long hours of labor, the privations in food, clothing, and shelter, and the hopelessness (E, II, 431; P, II, 611). But he rather hardheartedly supposed that such hardships were the consequences of the individuals' inherited natures and actions. He had insufficient appreciation, moreover, for the altruism toward each other of which working people were capable.

Spencer had the highest confidence that relative ethics, the adaptation of absolute ethics in given circumstances, would produce the greatest surplus of pleasure over pain in the long run. Conscience, the internalization of earlier political and religious sanctions, would long continue to coerce people (E, I, 127, 115 - 20; P, II, 598 - 602). But as provision for the future became more certain, people could increasingly subordinate simpler feelings to more complex ones. So they would begin to accumulate experiences of the remote pleasures of providence, justice, and beneficence, and of how pains were diffused to others by improvidence and aggression. As "inherited effects of such experiences" produced a "voluminous consciousness" of these consequences, people's desires would become the moral sentiments of freedom and altruism, and people would act spontaneously to increase life without any sense of obligation (E, I, 114, 121q., 129). When people fully adapted to society, when society fully evolved, and when population pressure lessened, individuals' participation in others' pleasures would begin to rival egoistic pleasures (E, I, 300). There would be no more misery, but smiles all around as every individual freely developed his or her different powers and looked for kindnesses to do or to allow others to do (E, II, 425; I, 252 - 55).

III *Altruism*

Spencer supposed that altruistic sentiments had become strong only with free labor in recent centuries (E, I, 239; P, II, 619). He allowed that self-sacrifice had occurred "from the dawn of life," but he restricted it to parents and offspring (E, I, 201).[18] This account of the development of altruism may be wrong. A recent study of altruism by a biologist, Robert L. Trivers, has made a strong case for the early development of moral sentiments. Reciprocal altruism gave an advantage in natural selection to those who, to their own apparent detriment, risked their lives for others and later became recipients of benefits themselves. Like self-sacrifice for kin (P, II, 599 - 600), reciprocal altruism was original, was prior to the development of friendship and sympathy, and was selected for individual, not group, benefit.[19] Moreover, "moralistic aggression"—indignation and hatred—might well have developed in reaction to "cheaters," those who did not return benefits. Spencer spoke of justice but never of moral outrage.[20] Trivers refers the development of social emotions to natural selection rather than to inheritance of the effects of past experiences. But he does not thereby delay, like Spencer, the take-off point for mankind's humanity to fellow man.

A contemporary scientist who had admired *Social Statics* and *The Data of Ethics*, Alfred Russel Wallace, also doubted that Spencer had accounted for "the advanced and enthusiastic *altruism*" that existed and had "always existed among men."[21] He contradicted Spencer's confidence that social evolution was progressive. Not industrial society, but communities of savages in South America and in the Orient showed some approach to Spencer's highest social state. True, they did not act only according to "an irresistible impulse to do" the right: they also obeyed public opinion. But they did live according to the law of equal freedom without "laws and law courts" and with only rare infractions of rights. In contrast, English society maintained "a mass of human misery and crime *absolutely* greater" than had ever existed before and left many "worse off than the savage in the midst of his tribe." Despite a few individuals, "the whole community" of English society did not have "any real or important supremacy over the better class of savages."[22] However wise Spencer was about the facts of men's egoism, his commitment to individualism does seem to have hidden from him how old, extensive, and strong, despite extreme privation, may be man's preference for cooperative, unselfish activity.

IV *Results*

The most important clue to the philosophical problems with Spencer's ethics is the determinism of *The Principles of Psychology*. There, although he granted that all were free to do what they desired, he held that desires were wholly determined by an "infinitude of previous experiences," most of them inherited in a person's "nervous structure" from "antecedent organisms" (P, I, 500, 502). With so many experiences influencing consciousness, one's feelings at any moment were incalculable, but their complexity suggested only an apparent freedom. Desires—"nascent excitations" of states of consciousness appropriate to an act—might be "changeable by volition"; but volition or will was "the unbalanced surplus of feeling of whatever kind" that determined action (P, I, 482; II, 463, 243). So one was not at liberty "to desire or not to desire," but only to do what one did desire. Spencer did not allow for the human capabilities to run changes on "those psychical connexions which experience [had] generated," and to generate new sentences contrary to what consciousness merely registered (P, I, 500). By making free will merely technical in his psychology, Spencer hid from himself the chief problem in ethics: giving reasons for feeling obliged to do something that we can think, for wanting what can be, for valuing the facts.[23] Instead, he pointed toward a day when people would not think of "must" or have any feeling of "ought," but only desire the good and act spontaneously (E, I, 128).

Accordingly, he did not see the need to provide arguments to persuade people to want to act on some desires rather than on others. Rather, he appealed only to what men in general have approved as "good" and explained the evolution of their desiring it.[24] Spencer assumed that the inherited consensus of mankind was sufficient warrant to make a principle scientific. He did not imagine that his principles must survive the test of falsifiability; he supposed they only had to be undeniable by the deliverances of consciousness. So in his ethics, he argued that since "preferences and aversions [were] rendered organic by inheritance of the effects of pleasurable and painful experiences in progenitors," everyone wished pleasure (E, I, 124). It did not occur to him that his task as a moral philosopher was to demonstrate that no one should *wish* to falsify the "moral intuition" that pleasure was good (E, I, 46). It was not enough for him to argue that as a matter of fact people called pleasure good; he needed to show why they were right to value pleasure.

His own procedure, then, accounts for why Spencer was disappointed that "the Doctrine of Evolution" did not yield better guidance than "right feelings, enlightened by cultivated intelligence," could give.[25] But after all, Spencer's ethics do contain the germ of a theory of morals. What he proposed amounted to "you ought to want more character, for then you will have more pleasure later, and that will establish more character, and so on." Utilitarian Henry Sidgwick objected that adaptation for survival did not necessarily yield more pleasure than pain—or as Spencer put it, "a surplus of pleasure somewhere."[26] But Spencer's point was that the surplus accrued in the benefits guaranteed to others by the individual's survival or to offspring by their inheritance of a better nervous system. Intuitionists could object that this reply clearly showed that pleasure was not an end, after all, but a regress. Yet Spencer the optimist assumed that people were not so bad that they needed a non-natural idea by which to evaluate their feelings.[27] He was well-intentioned; others were, too, and they all could follow his model: (1) The rules of conduct are (a) preferring complex feelings to simple ones, and (b) identifying with others' satisfactions when they are complex. (2) These rules produce happiness—more agreeable feelings for self and for others—in the long run. (3) I want happiness in the long run, since I have a character that is inherited and inheritable. (4) I had better conform to the rules of conduct. A twentieth-century difficulty is that character—a continuous identity—does not matter to people who have sufficient reasons to become 'different persons' in one or more of their social roles.

The fiercest contemporary objector to Spencer's ethics was his friend Huxley. Spencer was hurt that his scientific benefactor could call his political philosophy "reasoned savagery," and could not be reconciled to his friend for four years.[28] Huxley's "Evolution and Ethics" spelled out his key differences: his disbelief in the transmission of acquired characters, and his belief in the power of institutions—"laws" and "the state"—to civilize man.[29] He sided with Mill in rejecting instincts (and so inherited moral intuitions and sentiments) as guides for moral action.[30] Huxley's innuendo that Spencer was party to "the fanatical individualism of our time" was not a fair view of Spencer. Rightly or wrongly, he denigrated, as much as Huxley did, the instincts of savages, and also condemned the current, institutional "barbarians in broadcloth," from the hanging governor of Jamaica, Edward Eyre, to General Gordon (E, I, 474).[31] But Huxley's disagreement showed once again how much in Spencer depended on his view that the determining feature of human evolution was "the inheritance of functionally-produced modifications."[32]

Although Spencer's ethics were never philosophically reputable, Huxley was probably right that middle class and artisan readers gave the highest respect to language celebrating individual self-reliance.[33] Spencer's moral sentiment of equal freedom no doubt had strong appeal to such readers and especially to those who lived by a creed of personal success, aiming like Richard Potter at wealth and respectability.[34] The upper class might regard commercial ruthlessness as beneath their breeding; at least, Thackeray saw "hardheartedness and ingratitude" in broker John Osborne's falling out with his bankrupt benefactor, John Sedley.[35] But Spencer's view that all should accept the consequences of their conduct could take the curse off hardheartedness by representing it as justice in the long run. As long as most people's lives held more pain than pleasure, Spencer reasoned that "personal ends must be pursued with little regard to the evils entailed on unsuccessful competitors" (P, II, 611). It must have been agreeable for aggressive persons to learn that the pleasures of sympathy would often have to be sacrificed before the law of the survival of the fittest evolved generations who were more happy than miserable (E, II, 430 - 31).

CHAPTER 6

Biology

THE two volumes of *The Principles of Biology* (1864, 1867) were Spencer's most ingenious works. Darwin said of the one part supported by Spencer's own experiments, "it is wonderfully clever and I daresay mostly true."[1] Mill wrote that he was filled with wonder that Spencer's premises should be so explanatory of organization and life.[2] What Spencer attempted was to show that biological inductions like Darwin's could be explained by "universal laws of the redistribution of matter and motion."[3] From contemporary data of "gradual variation" of living things, Darwin had generalized "an analogous hypothesis" for a universal gradual variation of organisms in time (I, 494).[4] Spencer sought to go behind Darwin's theory by suggesting plausible physical antecedents for biological evolution. If the structures of organisms could be results of the first principles of universal evolution, then what Darwin called "accidental" or spontaneous variation could be reconciled with the Persistence of Force.[5] If for what Darwin called "our ignorance of the cause of each particular variation," "mechanical terms" could always supply causes for variation, then what was most disturbing about Darwinian evolution—its contingency, its randomness—could be accepted as part of a necessary, predetermined cosmic Evolution (I, 530q., 697).[6] According to his published plan, which he would follow also in his psychology and sociology, Spencer advanced through data and inductions to the leading aspects of the field of evolution—here, morphology and physiology. Of the final result, Darwin observed that "each suggestion, to be of real value to science, would require years of work"; but to a young biologist he wrote that Spencer was "the greatest living philosopher in England, perhaps equal to any that have lived."[7]

Spencer had given thought to the philosophy of biology for twenty years. Lamarck's theories of predetermined, progressive development first appeared for the general British reader in Lyell's geology and were seen there by Spencer in 1840.[8] Spencer never could say why he had accepted Lyell's account, rather than his refutations, of Lamarck's theories. One reason could have been Lyell's own support of the inheritance of acquired characters, an ancient idea that Spencer advocated two years later in *The Proper Sphere of Government.*[9] In *Social Statics,* he illustrated his political hopes of the eventual harmony of individual and society by reference to Coleridge's idea of life as the tendency to individuation, and by examples from biologists T. R. Jones and Richard Owen.[10] In 1851 on a walk with G. H. Lewes, he felt reinforced in his reliance on biology by learning of Milne-Edwards' idea of the physiological division of labor.[11] That year he studied comparative osteology (with Owen) and wrote his first argument for development by "continual modifications due to change of circumstances."[12] When Darwin saw it in Spencer's *Essays* in 1858, he praised it as "admirable."[13]

Most of Spencer's study of biology, including readings in Carpenter on physiology, went into his "Theory of Population Deduced from the General Law of Animal Fertility" (1852).[14] He proposed that self-preservation and reproduction varied inversely, since the coordination of actions that was necessary for extension of life diverted material (especially phosphorus) from germ cells to the development of a coordinating nervous system.[15] Among mankind, population pressure would continue to be "the proximate cause of progress" by requiring "a further enlargement of the nervous centre, and a further decline of fertility" in the "select" of every generation until the nervous system had no more to do than was natural to it and fertility levelled off. Thus, Spencer found biological cause for optimism in the survival, on the average, of people whose "power of self-preservation" was the greatest.[16] By emphasizing the survival of those who maintained life under population pressure and the elimination of those who did not, Spencer almost recognized natural selection. His explanations for missing the point were that in 1852 he thought the inheritance of acquired characters explained modification in living things, and that in 1852 he knew little about the phenomena of variation (II, 528 - 29n.).[17] But he also was not thinking about population pressure as Darwin had done after September, 1838. When he read Malthus' *Essay on Population* in that month, Darwin had adopted that pessimist's conception of life as an individual struggle for existence. Before that, like Spencer, Darwin had thought only that those animals survived, as a group, who could do so.[18] In 1852, Spencer's optimism was stronger than his individualism, and he never regarded the struggle for existence as significant for its individual effects until Darwin made his case from Malthus in 1859.

In the eight years before Darwin's book, Spencer, the former engineer, went his own way toward interpreting living things by physical principles. In two essays in 1857, "Progress" and "Transcendental Physiology," he attributed the development of organization from a homogeneous germ, to "agencies acting" and to "disturbing forces."[19] In both essays, physical conditions were the cause of habits, and these were inheritable by "the *only* law of organic modifications of which we have any evidence."[20] In 1858, "gradual differentiation" through inheritance of modifications brought about by "mechanical conditions, . . . muscular forces" was Spencer's alternative to Professor Owen's view that the vertebrate skeleton was specially (divinely) created.[21] In 1859, "The Laws of Organic Form" made symmetry dependent upon incident forces.

Spencer began *The Principles of Biology* in the fall of 1862 and devoted four and a half years to the two volumes. Huxley and Hooker read proof to correct mistakes in zoological and botanical facts.[22] Spencer drew many of the illustrations in Volume II and conducted microscopic investigations of the circulation of sap "before Darwin had begun his work on the movements of plants."[23] Later, Spencer felt that few parts of his work gave him "more pleasure in the execution" than Volume II; but at the time subscriptions to his philosophy were lapsing, and he was running out of funds.[24] Only an inheritance on his father's death and a gift of $7000 from American friends enabled Spencer to publish Volume II and continue his work.[25]

I *Volume I (1864)*

The first three chapters review the composition of organic matter and its interactions with physical forces. Spencer hoped to suggest some of the chemical inventory that preceded the origin of life, and he saw in colloids of large unstable carbohydrate and nitrogen compounds the likely sites for the earliest living things.[26] But by the doctrine of evolution through imperceptible gradations, he denied that any definite line separated inorganic matter from organic matter and the latter from the simplest living forms (I, 699, 702).[27] In 1898, he added a section on the chemical evolution which preceded the evolution of life; but he also decided that "Life in its essence" could not be conceived in physico-chemical terms, since "Ultimate Reality" was incomprehensible (I, 22 - 24, 120q.). He had no clue as to how living matter formed more living matter (I, 64). He did speculate that metabolism involved decomposition of phosphorus compounds in the chromatin of the nucleus, which triggered the decomposition of protein molecules, which in turn decomposed carbohydrate molecules (I, 260 - 63, 48). Although he supposed that it was impossible to conceive of life as emerging from chemical processes, he was on the right track, at least, since today "high-energy phosphate bonds" are regarded as the "sources of chemical energy" for cellular reactions that trap the energy of the sun (photosynthesis) and the energy in food molecules (I, 122).[28] Furthermore, molecular biochemistry promises to explain other processes that Spencer speculated about in terms of molecular interaction—muscle contraction and nerve conduction.[29]

The second three chapters originally began Part III of Spencer's psychology (1855). They developed the familiar definition of life—"continuous adjustment of internal relations to external relations"—into "the definite combination of heterogeneous changes, both simultaneous and successive, coordinated into correspondence with external co-existences and sequences" (I, 99 - 100, 107 - 10, 580). In 1898, Spencer granted that the definition gave only the "blank form" of life and not its content—activity (I, 113). For the latter, he retained his metaphor from *First Principles* of a moving equilibrium: a rhythmical movement of continual antagonistic forces, such as the course of a child's top or of the solar system (I, 110).[30] In a living organism, activity was always toward equilibrium of incident forces and physiological functions. By this reduction of the organic to an inorganic model, Spencer insufficiently recognized the behavior of organisms. Today the explanation of biological evolution is seen to be the differential reproduction that results from "the behaviour of all the individual organisms which compose a population."[31] Spencer was right, but not thorough-going in his revision for the activity of organisms.

Outstanding in Part II, "Inductions of Biology," and in Volume II were the explanations of Spencer's Law of the correlations of strength and weight and of surface and volume. Whereas weight (or mass) increased by the cubes of dimensions, the ability of muscles, bones, and plant stems, to bear strain, increased only "in proportion to the areas of their transverse sections" (I, 151).[32] Whereas size increased by the cube, the absorbing surface increased only by the square, of dimensions. By the second correlation, a large animal's heat loss from its surface would be relatively much less than that of a small animal (I, 152 - 53).[33] Also an increase in size would mean a relative decrease in surface that could absorb food until most organisms reached a point at which growth (cell-multiplication) stopped—"a state of moving equilibrium" (I, 152, 639).[34] From the first correlation, Spencer could explain the limits of weight in birds and of growth in land animals, as opposed to the size of whales and the growth according to food supply of animals like crocodiles and pike, whose weight was supported by water (I, 153 - 55). In Volume II, he could argue that development of the vertebral column and formation of wood were caused by alternate transverse strains exerted by muscles on the cartilaginous notochord and by wind on the lower part of the stem (II, 214, 220 - 21, 289, 345 - 46). Incident pressures would produce thickening until there was equilibrium; and with the inheritance of acquired characters, function could produce structure.

In 1864, Spencer declared the precedence of function to structure, but in 1898 he granted that they interacted at an equal rate. Whereas reaction to environment produced difference in structure, that in turn led to difference in function (I, 198).[35] An insight supported by later science was the view that in proportion as an organism counteracted environmental changes, it exhibited "greater unlikeness to its environment" (I, 176).[36] But the insight on which Spencer counted most to relate function and structure has found no scientific support.[37] He held that the structure of any organism was a "product of the almost infinite series of actions and reactions" to which ancestral organisms had been exposed. Any reactions by an individual, then, would "have but an infinitesimal effect in permanently changing the structure of the organism as a whole." Compared with all the preceding sets of forces, any reaction, even over many generations, would do but little to modify the inherited "moving equilibrium of functions (I, 242 - 43). Adaptation would be slow, a conclusion also at odds with modern genetics, which mathematically shows that a mutation can become established in a population in as few as ten generations.[38]

Imagining a glacial pace for hereditary change, Spencer nevertheless proposed an extremely sensitive mechanism for equilibrating local changes of function in the individual organism. Each organism would consist of and be structured according to the polarity of units "immensely more complex" than chemical compounds but smaller than cells (I, 226). These intermediate units would be all of one kind for each species, but they would be so complex that they could also bear individual traits.[39] Spencer modelled these "physiological units" after a contemporary explanation of immunity as an alteration of the molecules of the blood (I, 222). The specialized molecules of each organ would carry on repair by molding food materials into their own arrangement. Regeneration could occur because the physiological units of an organism, when not too specialized, could both arrange themselves into the form of the whole organism, and also "take part in forming any local structure under the influence of adjacent physiological units (I, 224, 364).[40] Assuming an unceasing circulation of protoplasm throughout an organism, Spencer supposed that "constitutional units" visited all parts of the organism. The results were an equilibrium of the polarities established by inheritance and by local functions, and an eventual gathering into sperm and egg cells of physiological units that carried the superimposed traits of local functions as well as the inherited constitution (I, 192, 319, 371).

Spencer compared the forces at work in this organic equilibrium to those maintaining the arrangement of the solar system. As the gravitation of each particle in the earth affected particles of the sun ninety-two million miles away, so "the excessively-unstable units" of organisms adjusted their polarities and structures into equilibrium with the forces within the organism that resulted from functional adaptations to external forces (I, 352).[41] Spencer was certain, by the "Persistence of Force," that differences of forces anywhere in the organism must produce differences in effects everywhere (I, 335). On this score, he finally declared that to say these effects were not inheritable was "indirectly to say that force does not persist." The arrangements of the components of the gametes would conform along with every part of the organism to any redistribution of forces in any other part of the organism (II, 394 - 95). Once again Spencer would recite his spell over matter and motion without considering whether in fact some effects were irreversible and so had no other outcome. In 1898, he did consider that as in the solar system, so in an organism, parts were "practically autogenous"; energies in each part caused effects "almost independent of the effects worked by the general energies (I, 366).[42] But this did not allow him to accept evidence for the germ-plasm theory of inheritance. His presupposition of "Cause" prevented him from entertaining any theory of inheritance that did not allow an uninterrupted multiplication of effects.

He did work wonders, however, with physiological units, to supply 'causes' for spontaneous variation. He argued that the numbers of units in reproductive cells must rarely be equal. From parents not constitutionally identical, then, "the small initial differences in the proportions of the slightly-unlike units" would lead to divergences from the parents in the mature offspring. Furthermore, in the embryo, incident forces would produce segregation of units from one parent in one place and of units from the other in another place, so that in the mature offspring some organs would follow the male parent, and others, the female parent (I, 330 - 31).[43] Finally, in the formation of reproductive cells, there would have occurred segregation and so a predominance of units derived either from the grandfather or the grandmother. So each fertilized egg would contain not only different numbers of parental units, but also different ancestral influences. From "these involved influences, derived from many progenitors," there would occasionally result combinations of units that would produce considerable and even wide divergences from the usual structures in the family and the species (I, 332). By natural selection of the most divergent forms, Spencer delivered what Darwin could not explain and so called spontaneous variation. It derived from "miscellaneously compounding the changes wrought [in phsyiological units] in different lines of ancestors by different conditions of life" (I, 334, 513). In 1898, he granted that "these unknown somethings" only served to generalize the phenomena of organization, and he reiterated that life was incomprehensible (I, 370, 373). But what he had done was to advance only the penultimate and most elegant version of the ancient idea of pangenesis: the collection in the reproductive cells of particles from all parts of the body. Darwin derived from Spencer his own notion of the inheritance of different gemmules from each organ of the parents, but the gemmules did not explain regeneration and abnormality so well as Spencer's theory seemed to do (I, 360, 362).[44]

When in 1898 he came to review the discoveries of mitosis and meiosis, Spencer thought that physiological units gave better explanations of cell organization and of fertilization than the accepted ones.[45] Since the nucleus was not geometrically central within a cell, he could not conceive how it could control the cytoplasm effectively (I, 258). He allowed that the nucleus might be a "stimulating centre," while it did not determine change in the cytoplasm. The "constitutional characters" (the units) would "inhere" in proteins throughout the cell (I, 260 - 64). Halving of the chromosomes in gametes (meiosis) was not the device that brought about fertilization. Rather, slight differences between physiological units produced the disequilibrium enabling anew the redistribution of matter and motion that constituted evolution of a new organism (I, 340, 295). Meiosis only signified the preconditions of sexual reproduction: "impoverishment and declining vigour" (I, 267). When such conditions halted asexual reproduction, natural selection established sexual reproduction with the available, reduced quantities of chromatin, the phosphorus of which continued to supply energy for the changes following fertilization (I, 264). Spencer did not know the fact that meiosis can precede asexual reproduction.[46] He also did not observe that his causal explanation of sexual reproduction was teleological. He argued that when organisms reached stable equilibria, they could no longer fertilize themselves: fertility depended on there being groups of slightly different units.[47] Sexual reproduction arose, then, because it was needed; organisms made a virtue of declining vigor. Spencer's explanation was no better than what he criticized in Lamarck: the "assumption of a persistent formative power inherent in organisms" (I, 492).[48]

Spencer came to this pass since he would not surrender his conception of germ cells as unspecialized and not fundamentally different from other cells (I, 283, 280). Since 1857, he had held that germ cells were uniform and homogeneous aggregates.[49] His definition of evolution called for an unstable homogeneity in which Persistence of Force could work a multiplication of effects. In his resistance to the correlation of chromosomes and hereditary characters, he shared the assumption of his time that inheritance was on the average a neutralizing or blending of characters (I, 332, 259).[50] But in oversimplifying the germ cell, he showed his characteristic wobble between mechanistic description and philosophical explanation.[51] By holding to his definition of evolution, even though it gave only "a rude conception" of the development of organisms (II, 242), he could not "cope with the very real and important sense in which a frog's egg or embryo is more highly evolved than, say, a grown-up earthworm."[52] He might account for the mature worm by heterogeneity and definiteness, but the heterogeneity of the frog's egg was inconceivable by his philosophy.

II *In Darwin's Territory*

Part III showed that Darwin and Spencer echoed each other on social evolution, the social significance of natural selection, the term "survival of the fittest," and use inheritance. Spencer objected to Darwin's reliance on the correlation of variations and reduced natural selection to a role subordinate to the direct action of external agencies.

Both men failed to distinguish between biological and social evolution. Neither saw that the latter process was not limited like the former to the time and space of only two individuals' heredity.[53] Spencer supposed that the descendants of Irish and German immigrants to the United States became Americanized by inherited modifications. The transmission of "the prevailing type" in a society by language was inconceivable to him (I, 310).[54] He could ask, "Until some beneficial result has been felt from going through certain movements, what can suggest [their] execution?" (I, 494). It never occurred to Spencer or to Darwin that innovation was available to every speaker through any sentence of his or her language.

Both men mistakenly saw natural selection as requiring a struggle for existence.[55] Darwin devoted a chapter to it, picturing "ten thousand sharp wedges packed close together and driven inwards by incessant blows" into the "yielding surface" of "the face of Nature."[56] Spencer the optimist gave a page to the warfare and carnage from the earliest times to the present (I, 425). Both men believed that biological evolution produced progress: "as natural selection works solely by and for the good of each being, all corporeal and mental endowments will tend to progress towards perfection"[57]; "slowly, but surely, evolution brings about an increasing amount of happiness" (I, 438). Both men refused to distinguish species from varieties by reproductive isolation; both focussed on "the formation of divergent organic forms" (I, 572).[58]

Spencer invented "survival of the fittest," and Darwin adopted the term as "more accurate" than "natural selection."[59] Spencer chose the phrase in June, 1864, as a "more literal" expression of natural selection as he explained it in physical terms: "a maintenance of the moving equilibrium of the functions in presence of outer actions . . . in contrast with the unstable equilibria of those which do not survive" (I, 548, 530).[60] Both men were insensitive to the misleading nuances of Spencer's phrase. It referred to the survival of individuals rather than to the fecundity of a population; and the superlative was inaccurate: the fit, not the fittest had most progeny.[61] Neither man supposed, moreover, that survival was only a probability, and that accidents did happen whereby the fit did not survive.[62] Spencer claimed that he meant "fittest to thrive under the conditions," and not "better"; but thriving could be either ability "to survive individually" or "higher degrees of fertility."[63] Because of his wish to study organic changes "from an exclusively physical point of view," he never saw clearly that it was the birth rate of a continuing wild species, not an individual moving equilibrium, that was selected (I, 431).

Spencer's master physical terms for the modification of organisms were "direct equilibration" of frequent but not injurious external forces by internal changes in function and structure; and "indirect equilibration" of destructive external forces by the survival of some moving equilibria that offered most opposing force (I, 528, 530). He derived the first process of functionally-produced modifications from Lamarck, but gave it priority, whereas Lamarck had regarded it as "the cause of irregularities" in the progress of living things (I, 496).[64] At first, Darwin refuted Lamarck by the evidence that the functions of sterile worker bees could never have modified the structure of the fertile bees who produced them; but later he allowed that use and disuse were causes of modifications (I, 560).[65] Neither man noticed the illogicality of expecting that a modification established through use in one lifetime could have an entirely different, self-starting origin in a descendant's life.[66] Although use may seem to mimic development, the fact is that individuals have genes that assist them to develop modes of behavior in their environments.[67]

Although Spencer protested often that he recognized the importance of natural selection, his efforts always went to reduce it from the primary to a secondary agency in the production of modifications. He allowed that protective organs were the effects of selection. But he also suggested that hairiness or hardness or oiliness that preserved more seeds of a plant, would have been the result of unusual nutrition and would depend upon "the same peculiarity of nutrition" in succeeding generations. Obliquely his argument implied more than it literally claimed. Spencer was really saying that natural selection preserved an "incidental peculiarity"; but direct adaptation to external agencies—soil, diet—provided the physiological basis for every peculiarity (I, 531 - 33, 540).[68] Natural selection could speed up—be an "accelerator" of—inheritance of acquired characters, but Darwin did "not recognize [use and disuse] to a sufficient extent" (II, 596; I, 535). Spencer did not appreciate natural selection as a fundamental hypothesis, but only as "a cause of divergence" that only furthered modifications.[69]

Accordingly, most of his treatment of natural selection was an attack on Darwin's finding that during growth and development "useful modification of one part will often have entailed on other parts diversified changes of no direct use."[70] Darwin's study of embryology and artificial selection had shown him that homologous parts tended to vary as a unit, and he emphasized development, not environment.[71] Without Darwin's knowledge, Spencer could not see from Darwin's argument how appropriate variations occurred simultaneously in muscles and bones (I, 537).[72] Rather than one variation at a time, the inheritance of functionally-produced modifications seemed a much more reasonable source for viable structures that, preserved by the secondary agency of natural selection, would become the head of the bison, the horns of the Irish elk or the moose, the giraffe's neck, the camel's hump, or the tortoise's shell. The only trouble was that Darwin even made correlated growth secondary to natural selection. Although he used Spencer, he showed in *The Expression of Emotions in Man and Animals* that the origin of behavior was not adaptation, since a common mechanism of nerves and muscles linked actions like laughter and grief.[73] Spencer's emphasis on the environment, rather than development, led him to envision organisms as being like "planets sweep[ing] on through a pathless void, in directions perpetually changed by gravitation." There were really no orbits and "survival of the fittest" was also "a figure of speech."[74] What really was perpetually going on, he wrongly thought, was "functional change demanded by some new external condition" and inherited by offspring (I, 540).[75]

III *Volume II (1867)*

Spencer's treatment of morphology and physiology in Parts IV and V was to assign physical causes for structures and functions (II, 224). He deduced differentiation of homologous units of any order from dissimilar relations to incident forces, since equal growth took place in directions where incident forces were equal (II, 159 - 60, 206).[76] Darwin quoted Spencer on differentiation almost immediately and remarked that without "facts to guide us, all speculation on the subject would be baseless and worthless."[77] Spencer continued to demote natural selection until it became the indirect abettor of "unlike incident forces on the aggregate of individuals, generation after generation" (II, 269).[78] So flowers developed, and the chief internal differentiation of plants—circulatory channels and layers of wood—were also the result of direct equilibration between inner and outer forces. Natural selection only preserved "inherited structures" resulting from "strains acting on successive generations of ancestral plants" (II, 290, 288).[79] So in animals, where strains also balanced along a neutral axis below the surface, there gradually differentiated epidermis, connective tissue, and vertebral columns (II, 210, 214). Either tissue adapted to external forces, or the moving equilibrium of the organism was overthrown. Repeated adaptation to persistent forces produced not only a new moving equilibrium, but also modification of tissues (II, 393, 290). So Spencer reached what he surprisingly called "the deepest knowable cause" of organic changes, the persistence of force. What had been in *First Principles* only an assertion of "Cause" and "an Unconditioned Reality," became knowable as an "ultimate fact" after the changes of form in organic tissue that Spencer imagined in Volume II (II, 393).[80] Meanwhile, he gave scarcely a word to the specifically biological components postulated in Volume I, the physiological units. Although they had seemed to be the causes of development, they and all other biological inductions turned out to be only the effects of physical causes and the results of persistent force.[81]

In the last part of Volume II, Spencer expanded the "law" of population that he had proposed fifteen years earlier. Again he sought to deduce from forces an idea that seemed reasonable to him: an antithetical relation of nutrition ("Individuation") to reproduction ("Genesis"). He did not consider that his philosophy might have offered a better explanation, a rhythm resulting from the two activities.[82] Instead, Part VI was a long exemplification of forces, involving not only Spencer's Law, but also profit and loss (II, 470, 501 - 02). Spencer recognized exceptions to his rule: by strength and cunning the omnivorous blackbird and rat attained large size without a lower birthrate (II, 503 - 04). Also, the more evolved organism might be absolutely less fertile; but because of superior nutrition relatively more of its offspring would survive (II, 505). Spencer granted that civilized men were more prolific than savages, but attributed that apparently adverse fact to easier self-preservation and relatively abundant food (II, 516, 520, 510). He still expected population pressure to develop the human nervous system, so that "greater emotional and intellectual power and activity" would become, "by small increments, organic, spontaneous and pleasurable" (II, 531). But he did not foresee zero population growth. Instead, he expected that changes in the physical environment—21,000-year climatic cycles of the hemispheres and geological changes—would prevent men from attaining "the highest life," "complete correspondence" with external relations (II, 534 - 35).

In his treatment of human biology, Spencer performed a lasting service in emphasizing the changeability of the species and hence, "human nature."[83] But his theory of population also showed his underestimation of humankind. "Nothing but necessity could make men" spend energy to gain "skill, intelligence, and self-control" (II, 527). People could not phrase and follow their own reasons for birth control. They would only work and provide higher education for children when compelled by an external force, pressure of population.[84] In arguing that individuation would decrease human reproduction, Spencer never noticed that it was not individuality, but self-awareness that distinguished mankind.[85] Having for decades a continuous reproductive capacity, humans have the highest reproductive efficiency among animals.[86] Even were there reduction in reproductive capacity as Spencer argued, it would not affect the human birthrate unless it approached "absolute sterility." Only people's giving themselves reasons for "voluntary family limitation," as they do for work and learning, could lead to a declining birthrate.[87]

IV *After Darwin*

Darwin died in 1882. In the last, sixth edition of *The Origin of Species,* he had added extensively to Chapter VII in defense of the principle of correlated growth. Although he could neither explain or predict it, highly complex transitions in structure did occur. In 1886, Spencer published "The Factors of Organic Evolution," a two-part attack on organic correlation and natural selection, in defense of use inheritance and the effects of external forces.[88] Rather than investigating the evidence either for correlation, or for transmission of functionally-produced modifications, he chose to argue about the giraffe's neck. He assumed that on Darwin's theory an improbable number of unrelated, lucky, spontaneous variations would be required.[89] That he was misreading Darwin occurred to him no more than that he was overlooking a cause of evolution in his own theory: the multiplication of effects. The inheritance of acquired characters had become a beam in his eye. In the second part of the essay, he made explicit the implication that he had left twenty years earlier: "external actions themselves initiate the structures." "Natural selection could operate only under subjection. It could do no more than take advantage of those structural changes which the medium and its contents initiated."[90] With Darwin dead, Spencer spoke out as Anti-Darwin. Darwin had insisted that environmental agencies were secondary and fortuitous; Spencer pronounced that they were "the primordial factor" and that natural selection was fortuitous.

When August Weismann published his germ plasm theory of inheritance in 1892, Spencer was "dreadfully disturbed." If there were from generation to generation a continuity of germ cells unaffected by adaptation, he feared that "the foundation of his whole philosophy [would be] undermined."[91] He wrote three essays in 1893 and one more in 1894 in refutation of Weismann and in defense of use inheritance.[92] "Right beliefs, not only in Biology and Psychology, but also in Education, Ethics, and Politics" depended on a "right answer" about the inheritance of acquired characters (I, 650). He reissued *The Factors of Organic Evolution* in 1895 with the prefaced argument that use inheritance allowed "institutions and circumstances" to mold people "far more rapidly and comprehensively" than natural selection alone could do.[93] This was a strange reversal of his position in his biology, where natural selection was the "accelerator," and "slow" use inheritance had "but an infinitesimal effect" in one generation and caused only little alteration in many generations (II, 596; I, 242 - 43).[94] There he had held that variations among civilized peoples might in "*a few centuries* show a considerable change," thanks almost entirely to *direct* equilibration (I, 553). One may wonder whether the deep, unadmitted disturbance for Spencer was that Weismann's theory would allow extensive organic changes in one generation. Spencer did not allow that institutions—people following routines—molded people culturally through language; the Irish and the Germans had to inherit their Americanness. Now a biologist was proposing variation in a manner that was inconceivable according to the Persistence of Force. How now could men progress to the civilized state in the "right," "slow" way that Spencer had conceived for them?

Spencer's chief arguments against Weismann, in any case, were that the germ plasm theory and negation of use inheritance were both inconceivable.[95] He found Weismann's theory unthinkable from his long unwillingness to observe in enbryology the facts of correlated growth. He produced negative evidence by imagining only "a fortuitous concourse of appropriate variations" (I, 671). The ironic result was that he put himself in the position of Richard Owen, who had supposed thirty-five years earlier that the only alternative to special creation was a fortuitous concourse of atoms. In 1858, Spencer had answered Owen that "gradual differentiations" could have produced the higher vertebrates (II, 565). In 1893, it was Spencer who demanded to know, like Owen, why differentiations occurred: why Amazon-ants could not feed themselves and how they became elaborately armored. On his own theory, he could offer "physical causes"—habits of being fed, and of being conquering ants (I, 670). He refused, as Owen had done against Darwin, to recognize correlation and natural selection as sufficient natural causes. Owen had insisted on supplementing natural selection by " 'derivation,' . . . an innate tendency to change."[96] Spencer insisted on the necessity of use inheritance, as well as natural selection, and found it "an incredible supposition" that natural selection explained what use inheritance might explain. After all, it was "impossible to imagine" how a germ cell could carry "the 480,000 independent variables required [by Weismann's theory] for the construction of a single peacock's feather" (I, 670, 695q., 372, 357).[97] Yet Spencer could imagine his own "incomprehensible" physiological units (I, 373). Would his perceptions have allowed him to conceive the two hundred thousand pairs of bases in the DNA of a mere virus? Spencer's arguments from inconceivability were always unlucky.

Weismann and Wallace showed to most persons' satisfaction that the negation of use inheritance was conceivable. Refusing to understand Weismann's metaphor of the immortality of germ cells, Spencer had invoked the "Law of Parsimony" against him (I, 640). A decade earlier, Weismann had agreed with Du Bois-Reymond that the theory of acquired characters was "only deduced from the facts which it attempt[ed] to explain." By the law of parsimony, it was an unnecessary hypothesis.[98] When all the possible cases of use inheritance suggested by Spencer had received explanation by the theory of natural selection, Spencer and others might still find reasons for use inheritance, but that "cause" was expendable.[99] In 1898, for example, Spencer tried to answer Wallace's point that natural selection accounted for the preservation of cave animals with smaller or covered eyes, since they would be less liable to disease. Spencer pretended that the point was liability to injury and cited the exposed eyes of the burrowing, blind crayfish. He also wrote ambiguously, "the eyes of these creatures living in darkness have disappeared from lack of use" (I, 309n.). This had been exactly Weismann's point against him: on the theory of use inheritance, visual organs should have disappeared completely, and they had not.[100]

The overall structure of Spencer's argument against both Darwin and Weismann was also fallacious: it amounted to an *ignoratio elenchi*. He argued as if he could prove that his own views were true by proving that their views were wrong.[101] He established neither proof and, as E. B. Poulton observed, ought to have applied "his acute intellect in testing" use inheritance in every possible way.[102] It is in his biology that Spencer most appears like George Eliot's Dr. Casaubon, speculating by the taper of his omniscience while he did not read the German and French scholars—say, Schwann and Bernard—who were advancing new models for the biological sciences.[103] Yet Spencer never felt himself to be lost, he completed his work, and he left some fascinating fallacies.

At a century's distance, it is interesting to notice that Spencer produced distortions and confusions by means of his definition of evolution. He neglected the differences between inorganic and organic evolution and the alternative phenomena not covered by his formula. The redistribution of matter and motion did not suggest to Spencer that inorganic evolution showed neither reproduction like biological evolution, nor self-transformation like social evolution.[104] Committed to defending the principle of continuity and to rejecting special creation, he relied on Persistence of Force and recognized no novelties. The origin of life, spontaneous variations, human innovation—all were to have been initiated by external forces and developed by slow organic change through use inheritance. Certain that evolution correlated with complexity, he overlooked the fact that not only complication, but also simplification, might be accompanied by specialization in function.[105] When evolution might both reduce and adapt the number of parts of an organism, then definiteness might be either an alternative, or a concomitant, to heterogeneity. Finally, the physical terms of his definition invited him to overextend the terminologies of the physical and behavioral sciences.[106] As a result, there were things that he could not see because of his terms. He extended physical models to the biological world, and the behavior of populations escaped him. He adopted a biological model for use inheritance and applied it—along with his physical model of the survival of the fittest as moving equilibria—to the social world. Consequently, he became blind to the "truism" that "the transmission of environmentally-induced traits to the next generation is just what does happen in *culture*."[107] In short, Spencer's definition oversimplified first his biology, and then his sociology.

Yet in the third quarter of the nineteenth century, Spencer's theories seemed most plausible.[108] He could seem both more philosophical and more precise than Darwin. He related biological development to a definition of universal evolution, and he offered mechanisms at almost every stage in his biology. Darwin's metaphor of "natural selection" was often misread to mean a selective power in nature rather than a natural law.[109] But "the survival of the fittest" seemed as clear as Spencer's Law on the relations of surface to volume and of size to weight and fecundity. Darwin followed Spencer halfway on use-inheritance, and their accounts of the uniformity of nature seemed more alike than they could after 1886. Even then Spencer's attacks on Darwin and Weismann won him the admiration of laymen for a while.

CHAPTER 7

Sociology

IN *Social Statics,* Spencer had stated the claim of his sociology: civilization was not artificial; it was a part of nature, "all of a piece with the development of the embryo or the unfolding of a flower."[1] In *First Principles,* he proposed the natural, cosmic process that would cause the development of societies: one evolution proceeding at all levels in the same direction, toward definite heterogeneity.[2] In his psychology and biology, he argued for the modification of mankind by the organization of ancestral experiences into nervous and other bodily structures which could be inherited. His sociology was to be an account of "super-organic" phenomena, the external and psychological conditions causing development of social groups.[3] His first full book in this field, a new one at the time, was *The Study of Sociology* (1873).[4] Full of "piquant illustration," it proved to be as popular as he had intended it to be and stimulated sales of his other books. In this textbook of general sociology, the most successful yet produced in England, Spencer outlined the breadth of sociology, counselled against biases in studying society, and advocated preparation in the sciences, especially biology and psychology, for the study of evolution in its most complex form.[5] He concluded by emphasizing a conservative significance for sociology in England. To last, English institutions and conceptions must be harmonious; any change in the social structure must be adapted to the average character of the people (SS, 360). It was not desirable that reform natural to more complex societies and less egoistic citizens should be widely accepted by the English people.[6] Their egoisms needed reform before institutions could be reformed. He looked forward to slow social change through the accumulation in human inheritance of the effects of innumerable actions by individuals (SS, 366 - 67, 108, 132).

I *Social Change*

One principle emerged from *The Study of Sociology:* the nature of the persons in a society (the "units") determined the nature of the society (the "aggregate") (SS, 46 - 47).[7] This key proved to be a fundamental weakness of Spencer's sociology, since he had no other conception of social relations except those between individuals and the aggregate.[8] He noticed, but he did not study property relations and authority relations (PS, II, 546, 572 - 73). He developed no conception like role, domain, network, or class, by which he might have interpreted the various actions of any individual.[9] As a result, in his sociology there appeared no explanations of functionally-produced modification in individuals' social behavior like those found in his ethics, psychology, and biology. The inheritance of acquired characteristics was assumed; how the units and the aggregate caused a social adaptation went unexplained (SS, 175, 307 - 08). In short, Spencer's accounts of social change lacked terms by which to correlate individuals' actions and social results.

In the perorations to both *Social Statics* and *First Principles,* Part I, Spencer insisted that individuals ought to try to effect social change by expressing their opinions: "[A person] must remember that while he is a descendant of the past he is a parent of the future, and that his thoughts are as children born to him, which he may not carelessly let die."[10] From the context, one finds that an individual was to utter fearlessly his or her deepest conviction or highest truth and to act on that belief whether or not the change aimed at could be brought about. But the expression of one's thoughts might not keep them alive, and if not, a person could not become a parent of the future. One might well think that it was Spencer who was careless how ideas were kept alive and how social changes were effected.[11] First he said that a person was "a unit of force, constituting, with other such units, the general power which work[ed] out social changes." Then he gave a simile that implied no social force beyond the parent and his children. Apparently, the disposition of ideas, let alone the organization of other potential social forces, would depend on random utterances and random acts. Any one person's responsibility stopped with the advocacy of an idea; no one needed to do more to affirm a thought. Yet the future and social changes would be worked out by each individual's leaving his or her utterance to have whatever effect it might.[12] One could suppose that the function of the simile was to dignify the concerned individual in the present (the parent) and to tie social change to the fate of ideas (the children) in the future. The simile would signify an intention to act—the parent of the idea—followed by an intention to deny having acted: the idea-children would be the actors. To benefit from social change, but not to accept responsibility for it was a state of mind with which many nineteenth-century writers were comfortable.[13] Not one of them was so confident as Spencer that there would be progress, that one could be unclear as to how, and that one could not expect it now, or quickly.

In *The Study of Sociology*, Spencer moved from "society" to "I" to "humanity" to "aggregate." "What, then, shall we say about a society? 'Do you think I am easier to be played on than a pipe?' asks Hamlet. Is humanity more readily straightened than an iron plate? [new paragraph] Many, I doubt not, failing to recognize the truth that in proportion as an aggregate is complex, the effects wrought by an incident force become multitudinous, confused, and incalculable, and that therefore a society is of all kinds of aggregates the kind most difficult to affect in an intended way and not in unintended ways—many such will ask evidence of the difficulty" (SS, 246). In the paragraphs before these, Spencer had argued that any law produced unexpected results. As the Reform Bill of 1867 had produced in the House of Commons "a raised sense of responsibility" to the working classes, so direct hammer blows to flatten the raised left edge of an iron plate would cause a warp near the right edge. He had suggested taking a planisher's advice: to rely on blows of varying force at various places, on indirect means, to effect social change. But talk of a "complex aggregate" is not a satisfactory explanation of society. There are, besides laws, other social forces which, by "variously-directly and specially-adjusted" actions leave multitudinous, confused, and incalculable effects.

The upper and middle classes are incident forces having such effects in the lives of working- and lower-middle-class people. Although few in number, they have at their disposal many sanctions, incentives, jobs, and offices which can motivate working- and lower-middle-class individuals to hope for favors, to separate themselves from their fellows, and to pretend that they are relying on self-help. Such influence was one of the indirect actions, along with higher real income, the patriotism of the Crimean War, and the rise of the Liberal Party, that straightened the left in the 1850's.[14] Yet Spencer gave no sign of remembering how he himself had spent 1848 in hoping and waiting first on the chance of Anglo-Indian patronage, so that he might teach in Bath, and then on the favor of Heyworth and Wilson. The word "aggregate" was the reflex of Spencer's negative estimate of social class as either an elite, or an occupation group, that had a bias, but that never was a force for social change. That he used so ugly a word so frequently was a sign that he needed its simplification of society as units of force summed and averaged.[15] "Aggregate" was sufficiently vague to seem to speak for itself and yet reflect the wisdom of its author.

II *Preparation in Biology*

It was surprising that Spencer credited Auguste Comte with having related the study of living things to the study of society (SS, 299). He owed some terms to Comte—"altruism," "consensus," "dynamic," "sociology"—but little more. The two founding fathers of sociology differed on virtually every topic, including biological evolution, so that it is a wonder that contemporaries found them similar.[16] Spencer owed far more to Milne-Edwards, from whom he read a physiology into the division of labor found in societies (SS, 305; PS, I, 452). In *The Study of Sociology,* he emphasized natural selection as a truth of biology that a sociologist must not disregard. It was the natural process for eliminating "good-for-nothings" from a society, and every artificial (institutional) suspension of the process lowered the society's moral and intellectual level (SS, 315, 313). He never saw the necessity of investigating whether these claims could be falsified.[17] He revealed that his approach to sociology from biology might not be very illuminating by an analogy between allowing the multiplication of the improvident and breeding from "worst-tempered horses" and "least-sagacious dogs" (SS, 337; PS, I, 70). So he began *The Principles of Sociology* (1876) by failing to make sufficient distinction between the societies of insects and of humans (PS, I, 5 - 6). Both were super-organic phenomena; insect societies, having only one parent each, simply never developed beyond being families. Preparation in biology never suggested to Spencer that the content and possibilities of human societies were unique because of people's intelligence and language.

Part II (1877) was the only section of Spencer's sociology directly based on biological analogies. By then he had been pursuing comparisons of society to living things for twenty-seven years.[18] He rejected Plato's and Hobbes' comparisons of the human body to society, and emphasized the analogy in organization of animals and nations—mutual dependence of parts.[19] He was fertile in finding ways to compare societies and organisms. Both grew in size not by simple increase in numbers of units, but by the compounding of groups of cells or of societies (PS, I, 465 - 67).[20] The stages of compounding had to be gone through in series before a tribe could become a nation (PS, I, 555). Spencer's Law applied: increase of mass brought increase of structure in organisms and societies (PS, I, 471). As late-evolved organs might develop early in the embryo of a much evolved animal, so in recent societies institutions might appear early that had been long in developing in older societies (PS, I, 484). Significantly, Spencer did not mark the contrast between unconscious tissue differentiation and conscious borrowing and planning of social arrangements.

The most important series of analogies extended through four chapters and compared the development of systems of organs in animals and nations (PS, I, Pt. II, chs. vi-ix). As the first tissue differentiation was of the skin from the alimentary system, so in nations there arose masters over slaves. As Spencer claimed that food taken in determined the features of the digestive system, so the resources of an area dictated the industrial activity in a society. With the specialization of its parts, there developed a vascular system in an organism. When division of labor in a society became specialized regionally, there developed a transportation network. Conflict with other organisms developed the nervo-motor coordinating system of an animal; war was the impetus to the organization of centralized government in a society. Finally, as sympathetic and vaso-motor nervous systems developed to monitor the inner organs and direct the flow of blood to them, so in a society there developed industrial and financial regulating systems.

Spencer was the first to point out two contrasts: in a social organism the units were not in close contact, like cells, but dispersed; and consciousness was not the concomitant of one system, but was possessed by each unit (PS, I, 460 - 61). Although like the life of the body the life of a society could continue when units of it died, the society could not, like the body, have any higher claim than those of its units. When such contrasts were turned against the analogy, Spencer insisted only on the parallel of a mutual dependence of parts and granted that it was only a "scaffolding" for the "sociological inductions" of growth by integration, differentiation of function, and development of structure (PS, I, 592 - 93). But his critics have replied that with or without the vehicle the interaction of size, function, and structure remained unexplained. Aspects of the division of labor in society were better understood than almost anything about a physiological division of labor. And in various societies, functions and structures differed in the authority or power that they carried. Spencer was really attributing to organisms what was still not proven of societies: that social structures were fully integrated and mutually dependent. Surely the three regulatory structures—state, market, and bank—had not developed the separateness called for by the analogy to organic systems. Moreover, they varied in time and in place in their dependence on each other.[21]

Spencer's analogy of society to an organism explained less and less as he elaborated it; but it was a euphemism that enabled him not to notice that he was skirting problems that his biology, sociology, and political economy could not have handled. The analogy would have been truer had it been drawn between an insect community and an animal body, but Spencer's biology could not have dealt with a discontinuity between animal and human aggregates.[22] He recognized that animal cells had been at work together for millions of years, whereas human units had been cooperating in higher societies for only a few hundred years. But he insisted that the character of a society still inhered in the character of all its units, for his sociology could not recognize the cultural hegemony of a powerful social group.[23] He could only account for differences in units by biological inheritance. But he could resort in good conscience, then, to an analogy from his theory of fertilization to explain degrees of stability in societies. Like organisms of different species, possessing mediately- or widely-different physiological units, peoples of strongly contrasting natures could not form entirely stable organizations. Such "hybrid societies" required coercion, whereas closely related peoples, like the "varieties of the Aryan race" in the United States, produced stable societies.[24] Finally, in one of his first uses of biological analogy, he could be comfortable in comparing circulations of coins and of blood corpuscles. His political economy would never have suggested to him that money did not actually flow, as blood did, to those units of the organism that were most active. By his analogy, he could avoid the consideration that the least replenishment for their labor trickled down to the actual builders of a railway.[25]

III *Preparation in Psychology*

Spencer advised the sociologist to consider the thoughts and statements of individuals as the motives of social change (SS, 349). Yet he had no clear notion of how these might aggregate, or of how feeling and purpose could work intra-subjectively in a social group—a work group, a team, a crowd, a class—to transform individuals' social relations and consciousnesses.[26] Rather, by the light of a premise of psychology, "the uniformity of historical change," he turned to prehistory for the sources of the greater part of the continuing (inherited) mental natures of men and women.[27] So in *The Study of Sociology,* he supposed that from women's role in reproduction had evolved not only an earlier stopping of physical development than in men, but also a lesser mental power. So he asserted lesser capacities in women for the most recent results of human evolution—abstract reasoning and the most abstract emotion, the sentiment of justice. He credited women's survival among men to an ability to please, to love of approbation, and to an ability, acquired through watchfulness, to anticipate male behavior. From women's relative weakness, he derived for them an admiration of power, a respect for freedom inferior to men's, and a loyalty to ceremonial or authoritarian aspects of society greater than men's.

It is not surprising that Spencer espoused such commonplace nineteenth-century views. It is his treatment of negative evidence, however—of how little was known about the many variables of prehistory—that is dismaying. One might well suppose that he would have recognized that there were too many variables and few facts known about them.[28] He admitted that he had only "entangled and partially-conflicting evidence," and that there were not "tolerably uniform manifestations of character in each race" (PS, I, 55 - 56). Still, he reduced the variables to his preconceptions about savages: impulsive and selfish, except as they were moved by their child-like love of approbation and their animal, sexual, and parental instincts.[29] Most implausibly, he decided that although animals might show sociality, the first people existed in isolation and unrestrainedly followed their immediate impulses (PS, I, 64).[30] In short, the social psychology he presented was based on a conventional, prejudiced analysis of primitive people. Received prejudices against women led him to believe their natures to be relatively primitive. His unexamined presumption that the unemployed were idle and improvident got "writ large in the savage."[31]

IV *Prehistory*

Spencer did not himself go "stamping out into the forest of prehistory."[32] He employed David Duncan (from 1867 to 1870), James Collier (1870 - 1877), and Richard Scheppig (1872 - 1875), to digest for him books on uncivilized and civilized peoples.[33] He had long regarded "Descriptive Sociology" as "the only history . . . of practical value," and from 1873 to 1881 he published eight volumes of ethnology tabulated by his three readers.[34] The work broke the health of Scheppig and of Collier, who emigrated to New Zealand, and Duncan and Scheppig took teaching positions in India and Germany.[35] Spencer paid their living expenses and was to divide with them the net returns from sales of the *Descriptive Sociology*, but the series did not sell.[36] Spencer covered nearly half of his losses by his profits from *The Study of Sociology*, was spared work constitutionally impossible for him, and was able to cite examples from hundreds of titles in each volume of *The Principles of Sociology*.[37] In Volume I alone, "there were 2192 references to the 379 works quoted," and in the third edition (1885), "about 2500 references to 455 works," according to Henry R. Tedder, Librarian of the Athenaeum Club, who verified all of Spencer's quotations for him.[38]

Surely the preparation for Spencer's sociology was one of the wonders of nineteenth-century scholarship. Spencer's selection of titles and his use of the compilations that he paid for, however, were less scholarly. It is true that most of the titles available to him were travel books. But through all three volumes, he interpreted sources of the "most uneven merit and incompatible orientation" according to preconceptions that were ordinary in his time, but that were beginning to be questioned.[39] He might have been more critical.

Spencer deduced most of Part I, "The Data of Sociology," from the improbable premise that the laws of thought were the same everywhere. The method of the savage mind was like that of the civilized mind: it classified objects and relations by likenesses (PS, I, 100, 107). Early people found false and inconsistent likenesses, but they were as scientific as they could be, given their limited practice of analysis. They saw changes in water, plants, animals, and people and believed in metamorphosis (PS, I, 111). They saw living things simulate inanimate ones—as in losing and regaining consciousness—and believed in a double, like a shadow, which could depart from a body and return to it (PS, I, 143, 117). So they developed funeral rites, to encourage the spirit to return to the inanimate body, then to provide for the spirit, and then to worship an ancestral spirit (PS, I, 282 - 83, 294). They transformed ancestor worship into worship of deities. Animal worship originated in people's mistaking the metaphorical animal nicknames of ancestors and heroes as, first, literal animal ancestors, and then totems and deities (PS, I, 343 - 54).

The theory which Spencer proposed discredited the theory of innate ideas of deity, by finding the source of every religion in ancestor-worship (PS, I, 368, 421 - 22). But fear of the dead was not in fact the only religious emotion, and ancestor-worship was neither universal, nor the sole content of any one religious cult.[40] By reducing variables, Spencer could spin out a theory. It would have been a truer theory had he recognized the need to study the psychology of a group in a definite social situation. Primitive peoples, peoples of other cultures, must think in the forms of their languages, which do not necessarily follow Indo-European classifications of content and form like body-double and ancestor-worship.[41] The realms of magic and mana were important to primitive peoples; but the first got barely mentioned in Spencer's account, and the other was by definition unclassifiable and unknown to Spencer (PS, I, 244).[42] The awe with which people revered a sacred power in a person or thing was not like the presupposition of causality which Spencer invoked as the Persistence of Force. Although the awe and the presupposition both might support unscientific expectations of impossibilities, they were opposite laws of thought.

Spencer was so busy with his psychology and sociology that he did not notice that E. B. Tylor had anticipated his ghost-theory in two articles before his own "The Origin of Animal-Worship" (1870) and Volume I of his sociology (1876). When Tylor accused him of plagiarism of his evidence for the double from shadows, reflections, echoes, dreams, suspensions of consciousness, and death, Spencer was dumbfounded.[43] Of course he had not read Tylor's articles; he had been using David Duncan's work. But he could only explain the similarities which included even the order of the items, by appeal to the order of evolution—inorganic to organic, simple to complex, and general to special. And for failing to cite Tylor's *Primitive Culture* (1873) when he spoke of "object-souls," he could only say that he had listed the title in the bibliography of Volume I (PS, I, 180).[44] As Tylor said, it was an "unpleasant controversy": Spencer showed so little sense of his responsibility to do justice to the equal claims of another individual in the field.[45]

In Part III, "Domestic Institutions," Spencer reduced variables, so as to move from the simple to the complex, by supposing that the first groups of primitive people had no family relations except those of brutes (PS, I, 622). Promiscuity was prevalent, matriliny was usual, women were brutalized, and children rarely survived (PS, I, 647, 650, 762). Kinship groups preceded larger aggregates, and universally polyandry and then polygyny preceded monogamy. In proportion as a society was more peaceful, there developed higher domestic institutions and improvement in the status of women (PS, I, 622, 692, 743). When men did not go to war, women's occupations could become almost the same as men's, and as a result their social position would be "relatively good" (PS, I, 734). Spencer was wrong in all of these findings, since he underestimated the earliness and specialness of primitive societies. The prevailing view reporting promiscuity was untrue, and society preceded kinship groups. Marriage relations and kinship systems evolved specifically within each society. Monogamy was often early, and matriliny often did not develop.[46] Spencer aimed to show that social evolution followed his general definition, and that it supported his theory of ethics. The ethic of the ancient unit of society—generosity—ought not to be the ethic of modern society, whose unit was the individual, not the family (PS, I, 714, 770). As Spencer argued in his politics and ethics, justice according to the law of equal freedom should be the rule for modern political institutions.

V *The Evolution of States*

Spencer claimed that the facts of the *Descriptive Sociology* demolished or greatly altered his prejudgments of despotism, slavery, and ecclesiasticism as social evils.[47] Despite George Eliot's appeal that he finish his ethics after *The Data of Ethics* (1879), he turned back to writing his sociology with a sense of urgency. He found that Nonconformists, "leading working-men," and unbelievers were opposed to the Government's "return to militant activities." He thought it was important both "to move" politically, as he did two years later, and to deal with the political aspect of social evolution.[48] What he offered in Parts IV, V, VI, on Ceremonial, Political, and Ecclesiastical Institutions was an account of the establishment of almost all societies by war and the domination of conquering peoples. He did not, however, gain his leading ideas—and he acknowledged that only his large conceptions would be especially clear—from facts new to him (PS, I, 243). Twenty-five years earlier, he had approved Carlyle's teachings that slavery had been a useful discipline and that the will of the strong man had ruled the earliest social groups. And he had argued then that government and religion began with a chieftain who was deified and whose sons became his political successors and chief priests.[49] His new idea in 1877 was that ceremonial control was the earliest and most general kind of government.[50] He presented ceremonies—the badges of honor and the marks of dishonor—as the characteristic social bonding developed by the individuals in a militant society.

In Part V, he claimed that he would be almost dispassionate in contemplating how the slain and slaves advanced the development of social structures (PS, II, 231 - 32). But almost immediately he wrote a sarcastic footnote on the shelling of an African town by three English warships, an act which the *Times* had found "somewhat humorous." Spencer remarked, "Comments on Christian virtues, uttered by exploding shells, may fitly be accompanied by a Mephistophelian smile" (PS, II, 239 - 40n.). Two pages later, in the large print, he was concluding that "the struggles for existence between societies have been instrumental to their evolution":

> Inconceivable as have been the horrors caused by this universal antagonism which, beginning with the chronic hostilities of small hordes tens of thousands of years ago, has ended in the occasional vast battles of immense nations, we must nevertheless admit that without it the world would still have been inhabited only by men of feeble type, sheltering in caves and living on wild food.
>
> . . . While conceding that without these perpetual bloody strifes, civilized societies could not have arisen, and that an adapted form of human nature, fierce as well as intelligent, was a needful concomitant; we may at the same time hold that such societies having been produced, the brutality of nature in their units which was necessitated by the process, ceasing to be necessary with the cessation of the process, will disappear. While the benefits achieved during the predatory period remain a permanent inheritance, the evils entailed by it will decrease and slowly die out (PS, II, 241 - 42).[51]

It is difficult to follow the expectation that in the long run only the benefits of war would be permanent, especially since Spencer later held that social life during war was demoralizing (PS, II, 640). That his feelings were at odds with his need to reduce variables was evident five chapters later. He first left "open the question whether, in the absence of war, wandering primitive groups could ever have developed into settled civilized communities"; and then two pages later he decided, "only by imperative need for combination in war were primitive men led into cooperation" (PS, II, 362, 365).

The leading ideas of Part V were findings about political differentiation and integration. The origin of the former was the formation of the first "two political classes of rulers and ruled": men and women (PS, II, 289). Political organization always involved the people, the chief, and the leading men. Headship, command that must be obeyed, was essential at first, but was checked by efficiency until it became settled by inheritance (PS, II, 312, 348, 363 - 65). Spencer had completed Chapters xvii and xviii, contrasting militant and industrial societies, just before he began his work in the Anti-Aggression League in the fall of 1881. He regarded those chapters, and especially "The Industrial Type of Society," as "culminating . . . the Synthetic Philosophy, in so far as practical applications are concerned."[52]

Spencer drew static contrasts between two types of aggregates and between the resulting character traits of their units. Ancient Egypt, Sparta, Rome, Incan Peru, Czarist Russia, and Prussia were militant societies. There the society owned the individual and controlled him by a central administration that tended to be despotic and by a chain of command. Status, rank in one of the hierarchies of the society—the army, the church, the civil government—determined social relations. All of the hierarchies regimented, prescribed the daily activities of the individuals they controlled. Compulsory cooperation was the rule and channelled individuals into their fathers' occupations. Only small, coercive private associations, such as guilds and secret fraternal societies, could be in keeping with the state structure. The goals of the society were political and economic autonomy (PS, II, 572 - 77). Through survival, there developed characters in the citizens that revered bravery and admired patriotism, faith, loyalty, and obedience. Social sympathies were checked by callousness to suffering. Vengeance pursued against foreign enemies led to revenge-taking within the society. Peaceful occupations, including intellectual pursuits, were scorned, and belief in great men and supernatural beings retarded the development of the sciences (PS, II, 594, 599).

Nineteenth-century Britain came closest to Spencer's ideal—industrial society. But it was a "compromise between militancy and industrialism"; and with the current retrogressive movement for military adventures and government regulation, a separation of the parts of the compromise was not feasible. Nevertheless, he looked forward to a renewal of unimpeded industrial development (PS, II, 537, 660, 618). This would mean an emphasis in the society on voluntary cooperation, not only or necessarily on industriousness. The society would exist to defend the individual, but government would be only negatively regulatory, limiting individuals' encroachments on others. There would be no public aid; the superior in the industrial struggle for existence would thrive. Contracts, drawn according to supply and demand, would determine all important social relations. Every variety of private association could exist, and social organization would be plastic, since individuals by their efficiency could acquire occupations other than their fathers'. The goals of the society would be free trade and at least an international federation of governments (PS, II, 604, 610 - 15). Character traits of units would be independence and diminished patriotism, faith, loyalty, and obedience. Individuals would honor civilians and condemn revengefulness. Since peaceful occupations would not require "aggressive egoism," individuals would become less unjust and more philanthropic (PS, II, 632 - 37, 640q.).

Spencer was not aware that he was contributing to a traditional topic, the contrast between civil and military societies.[53] He also did not observe how his scenario for primitive peoples led him to ignore the heterogeneity—by his own definition, the high level of social evolution—possible in primitive societies; and to see uniformities, rather than heterogeneities, in his types of societies. He held that most primitive societies were militant, although he granted that some were peaceful and unmarked by rigid subordination and status (PS, II, 631 - 32, 235).[54] But his characterization of primitive people did not suggest to him that they could develop social structures that called for either cooperation or competition. He assumed that only from peremptory need did primitive people cooperate, and that only from the discipline of command did they evolve the capability for voluntary cooperation or competition. From the same underestimation of humans, it did not occur to him that both cooperative, and competitive, societies could foster "strong ego development." So he missed the point that achieved status would be as important to individuals in a competitive society, as caste status could be to members of a cooperative society.[55]

It has proved difficult to see how a militant society could evolve into an industrial society. Without any "mechanism of causation," Spencer's sociology has seemed to allow only for more powerful militant societies.[56] In fact, the militant society has seemed much more like a social organism than the industrial, or as Spencer's type has been renamed, the open society.[57] Finally, twentieth-century industrialized societies have shown various combinations of the features of Spencer's two types. In every one, hierarchies manage the society, and individuals pursue status. In the West, there are military-industrial complexes, and many obstacles to social mobility are set at birth. In the East, there is compulsory cooperation, but it is accompanied by education emphasizing advancement of the children of efficient workers. In short, Spencer's two types do not describe social evolution. And they do not even present uniformities rather than definite heterogeneity.[58]

The institutions treated in Parts VI and VII were derivative. The priesthood developed to carry on the worship of deified rulers; and the professions, to serve the designs of church and state. Although he presumed that the savage's traits were anti-social, Spencer showed unusual respect for the usefulness of traditional beliefs, of priesthoods' insistence on obedience, and of asceticism's teaching the postponement of gratification (PS, III, 106, 142 - 43). He continued, however, his youthful charge that the clergy of the Church of England did not denounce what they ought, whereas "dissenting ministers, derived from classes engaged in . . . industrial activity, [were] the least militant of religious functionaries" (PS, III, 148, 117q.)

Spencer's recommendations for cooperatives occur in the last part (1896), on industrial institutions, and will be noted in Chapter 8. In the last stage of his account, he reaffirmed of "social progress" what he had observed twenty and even forty years earlier: evolution was "not linear but divergent and re-divergent" (PS, III, 331q.; SS, 300).[59] Although by reducing variables, Spencer left orthogenetic accounts of the types of marriage and society, his general views were better. Evolution was not "inevitable . . . , or even probable" in every society. At the beginning and the end of his sociology, he held that only "the entire assemblage of societies" would fulfill his definition of evolution by showing "increase of heterogeneity" (PS, I, 96; III, 610). His attempt at figuring general social evolution has found favor with theorists of developing and industrialized societies.[60] He has been regarded as an initiator of two viable perspectives: that industrial society is inherently peaceful, and that plant and animal ecology are important for man's existence (PS, I, 10 - 11). Most importantly, Spencer the sociologist was the creator of functionalism, the study of the effects for a society of what people do, not what they intend. So, for example, "conditions and not intentions determin[ed]" whether a society had one ruler or several leaders (PS, II, 395q.).[61] Finally, Spencer's ideas had several decades of influence in American social sciences after 1880, and later work was defined against his Lamarckism, his view of primitive people as children, and his view of ecology as a factor in social evolution.[62]

The great weakness of Spencer's sociology, on the other hand, was its underestimation of what people achieved, not in spite of, but through their purposes. By language and cooperative labor, people create purposefully their goods, knowledge, and laws. Although many social consequences involve so many interactions that individuals' intentions are of a gauge too fine for description, in many ways people do consciously plan a continuing social life.[63] Although Spencer tried to defend his completed sociology from the charge, it did slight the psychology of social life.[64] He had promised, but did not begin three more parts of his sociology on lingual, intellectual, and aesthetic progress.[65] His conceptions of law and of language were rudimentary: "the rule of the dead over the living," and a reporting ("inter-nuncial") instrument (PS, II, 514; I, 460). From his appreciation for music he had written of it as a language for the feelings, but he did not perceive how people used their language to grow and to transmit their human, social way of life.[66] He adopted uncritically the conventional ideas of his time about language. So his views of language blocked him from gaining a grasp of culture.[67] He assumed that languages become more complex; actually there is no overall movement even toward simplicity in grammar.[68] He supposed that the languages of early and non-European peoples were imperfect and undeveloped like the speech of a two-year-old. Savages spoke "a language containing only nouns and verbs."[69] Actually every language operates with a vocabulary and rules for naming agents of action, for expressing action, for qualifying both, and for forming an infinite number of sentences.[70] Spencer emphasized only that language could facilitate communication and perpetuate error. So the "inadequate" vocabularies of early or primitive peoples led to "indefinite" metaphorical statements from which arose the misinterpretations, the "linguistic errors," that encouraged worship of animals, plants, and places (PS, I, 136, 370 - 71). Actually, every language is adequate for the culture of its speakers, and their language demonstrates to them the adequacy of their culture.[71]

CHAPTER 8

Economics and Political Philosophy

ECONOMICS and politics were the fields of Spencer's work which his philosophy of evolution affected least. Almost all of Spencer's political philosophy came out of *The Proper Sphere of Government* and *Social Statics*. Later essays, *The Man 'versus' the State*, *Justice*, and *The Principles of Sociology* reiterate, clarify, and generalize the individualist theory and anti-government practice recommended in the first two books. In his political feelings, Spencer's course was from hopefulness of rapid improvement in "this transition state of ours" between savage and social life,[1] to resignation that institutions could only change as the character of individuals slowly improved. In his later years, his certainty that social evolution would be very gradual led him to retract his early support for communal ownership of the land, suffrage for workers and for all women, children's rights, and the right to ignore the state. He never deserted his abstract individualism or his trust in the "natural" economic laws of classical political economy. He persevered in his criticism of bureaucracy, but was never led by it to distinguish society from the state. Indeed, because of his devotion to his early economic and political ideas, he did not quite grasp the evolution in his time of the economy and parliamentary politics of Britain.

In *Social Statics*, Spencer first spun out at length his views on ethics, economics, and politics. A review of the organization of Spencer's first long book will explain why most of its topics have been reserved for this chapter. Spencer's introduction and first six chapters aimed to establish a first principle of ethics for government; the following twenty-six chapters argued specific applications in economics and politics. Spencer first rejected empirical Utilitarian ethics on the grounds (1) that people could never know enough to calculate the consequences of their acts as the Utilitarians proposed to do, and (2) that human nature was both indefinitely variable and improving, not uniform and simple as the Utilitarians supposed it to be. He accepted instead the premise of intuitive ethics that people had an innate moral sense, which he saw as guiding them toward the realization of the divine Idea, man's happiness. Spencer proposed that people had an instinct of personal rights that led them to claim exercise of their capabilities as their natural right. From sympathy for others, they had also developed a sentiment of justice that led them to respect others' claims. These two impulses, urging one's own and others' claims, should teach everyone the only correct rule for social relationships: each person had freedom to do his or her will, providing that another's freedom was not infringed. Beyond this proviso, restriction of one's own or another's will was a matter for private, individual judgment and was not within the province of government. In this chapter, the significance of Spencer's early and later views on economics and politics will be discussed; Chapter 5 has already shown how his evolutionary ethics were a revision of the intuitive ethic of *Social Statics*.

In 1892, Spencer revised *Social Statics*, dropping much on ethics that he considered to be better treated in *Justice* (1891), Part IV of *The Principles of Ethics*, and adding a principle to harmonize his political philosophy with his system of philosophy. This principle was the conversion and conservation of energy, which in *First Principles* and *The Principles of Psychology* Spencer had extended from physical events to mental ones. In the new *Social Statics*, he identified "moral feeling" as a force just like any physical force and argued that social conduct could no more be multiplied by government than any new physical force could be created by man. Though he claimed this was "as true in ethics as in physics," Spencer was repeating his error of extending the principle of continuity from matter to mind until all collapsed into Persistence of Force.[2] This time his identification of all forces aimed not at explaining the inheritance of acquired characteristics but at saving the phenomena of self-help, which he valued as the highest social conduct. The best politics would leave individuals to accept as well as they might all of the consequences of their attempts to adjust to their society. A society would improve if the government did not interfere with the survival of those individuals who made the fittest adjustment to society in each generation.

I *The Unsophisticated Laissez-Faireist*

Spencer never wrote an introduction to political economy, and there is no evidence that he ever studied economics. Nevertheless, he believed that through commercial liberty and unlicensed competition, social progress would spontaneously and naturally occur. In *The Proper Sphere of Government*, he had affirmed "a beautiful self-acting principle" keeping society "in equilibrium" while man worked "to secure his progression."[3] In *Social Statics*, he surmised "a gigantic plan," whatever is is slowly growing perfect: "Always toward perfection is the mighty movement—toward a complete development and a more unmixed good, subordinating in its universality all petty irregularities and fallings back, as the curvature of the earth subordinates mountains and valleys." His own political practice, his uncle's example and conversation, and the kindred views of James Wilson, editor of *The Economist*, sped him on to his own exultant conclusion that people were improving in morals and making progress towards less government and fullest liberty. Public opinion was "the new style of government," replacing force; and benefit societies, associations, and joint-stock companies were the new agencies replacing arms of the state (S, 14).[4]

Most remarkably, Spencer looked forward to the dispossession of landowners. Eight years before he had defended property in land, though it were "seized by the few," at the same time that he had rejected a Poor Law as indirectly harmful, prolonging the causes of poverty (P, 7, 12). Now he argued that exclusive possession of the soil directly infringed on the equal freedom of landless people to exercise their faculties, since they could only exist on the earth with the landowners' consent (S, 104). As man's social development had brought recognition that killing and enslaving people were crimes, so man would learn to regard depriving "others of their rights to the use of the earth" as a high crime and would settle fairly the claims of the landowners. Then all men would be free to bid to lease land from the nation (S, 111-13).[5]

Thomas Hodgskin—deist, laissez-faireist, early critic of political economy, and an editor of *The Economist*—opened his library to Spencer while he was writing *Social Statics*. Hodgskin's wife told his daughter that Spencer was "one of those men who made good use of your father's brains and knowledge as well as of his books."[6] The ideas in *Social Statics* that show affinities with Hodgskin's ideas were, however, already visible in *The Proper Sphere of Government*. Moreover, Spencer never showed that he learned anything from, or even of, Hodgskin's most original ideas. When Spencer knew him, Hodgskin was a deist who located God's design—"the progressive improvement of individuals and nations"—not in the existing society but in natural laws.[7] Nature, for Hodgskin, included the rights of men, as arbitrated by God's gift of a moral sense, and his own version of classical economics.[8] In *The Proper Sphere*, Spencer had insisted upon "man's natural rights," had held that by "his Creator" "man was created a progressive being," and had attacked, as Hodgskin did in *The Economist*, state regulation of commerce and provisions for health, education, and welfare (P, 5, 25).[9] The two both owed much of their talk of God to William Paley's natural theology, but Hodgskin was surely the more convinced deist.[10] Spencer was eclectic: he used Paley on the expedient to defend property in land in *The Proper Sphere*; in *Social Statics* he chose, without acknowledgement, Paley's definition of happiness, the "exercise of our faculties" (P, 14).[11] Hodgskin expected that justice and happiness would develop when each individual took full responsibility for himself; when legislation ceased; and when a harmony of economic interests became established through free and fair trade of commodities.[12] Spencer had asserted the first in *The Proper Sphere*; and in *Social Statics* he continued to retain the state for the administration of justice and to regard classical economics as an unexamined given.

He would have done well to have learned economics from Hodgskin. Spencer was naive to suppose that his laissez-faire view of industrial capitalism could be consistent with his labor theory of value.[13] Unrestrained competition did not yield the worker benefits equal to the worth of his labor to the capitalist. Yet Spencer held to the "Manchester" view that the competitive exchange value was the worth of labor.[14] Hodgskin's revision in economics was to point out that wages were not paid out of a fixed fund of capital accumulated and reserved by capitalists to pay wages, but from the goods being produced by "co-existing labour."[15] All wealth for production—fixed and circulating capital—derived from "present labour."[16] The capitalist "appropriat[ed] to himself" the "larger share" of "the labour of some men" and so was "enabled to *support* and consequently employ other labourers."[17] A natural, rather than an artificial, law of property would enable all labor—whether by master, journeyman, merchant, or farmer—to enjoy all of its product.[18]

Had Spencer learned to hope like Hodgskin for that result, *Social Statics* could have been even more hopeful about individuals' opportunities. He could be a perceptive observer of deprivation, but according to his economics he could see no remedy. He read Henry Mayhew in the 1849 *Morning Chronicle*. He knew that pieceworkers were sweated; that those workers were not idle, but hardworking (S, 207n., 311; PS, III, 569).[19] Later he acknowledged that the "wage-earner" was "temporarily in the position of a slave" and that workers could be "used up" in "commercial struggle." But he supposed that workers' imprudence, their "multiplying in excess of the means of subsistence," meant there could be "no remedy," and that the suffering, the loss of human possibilities, "must be endured" (PS, III, 573, 525; S, 289 - 90). Had he recognized with Hodgskin that an individual's command of other individuals' labor makes possible an infringement of their rights, he could have seen that capitalists as well as landlords have power of consent over workers' existence on earth. He could see that landlords' command, through revenue, of the labor of many servants, deprived society of wealth-producing labor (S, 210n.). Had he learned from Hodgskin how to apply consistently the labor theory of value, he could not have miscalculated the cost of resuming public possession of the land. Instead, he supposed that rents had not compensated landlords for two thousand years' investments (E, II, 91 - 92, 442 - 44).[20] A little learning from Hodgskin and he would not have lost hope of people's obtaining their right to the use of the earth. He then could have avoided Henry George's attacks, which so embittered his last years.[21] George *had* learned from Hodgskin that landlords would have received the value of their improvements from others' labor, and also made short work of Spencer's failure to count rents inflated by population increase.[22]

But Hodgskin, a laissez-faireist himself, could not have taught Spencer to see with the eyes of another school. James Hole might have done so, had Spencer read his *Lectures on Social Science*, which John Chapman published along with *Social Statics* in 1851. Hole, a clerk in Leeds, was a supporter of various cooperative associations and of education for working people. In his book, he argued that "the present plan, or 'no-plan' " (Hodgskin and Spencer spoke of the Divine plan) led "the machine-assisted laborer *alone*, [to have] to be prevented from employing his child of nine years for fourteen hours a day, nay twice, or thrice that period, without intermission" (S, 118).[23] Spencer gave no attention in *Social Statics* to child labor, a touchy issue with *The Economist*, which had opposed the 1847 Ten Hours Act. Machine production, calling for unskilled detail labor, both caused unemployment for skilled workers, and thereby forced employment, at even lower rates than otherwise, of unskilled women, girls, and boys. Spencer could live several years as a boy near Nottingham, yet because of the workers' isolation from middle class families he would never recall it as a region notorious for its lace-mending children who worked to early deaths by consumption.[24] Had Spencer learned from both Hodgskin and Hole, he might have seen how capitalists' command of labor caused not only inadequate earnings, but also constant unemployment.

Hole pointed out that capitalists' command of the labor of many servants deprived workers of productive employment.[25] The capitalists were not living abstinently, but rather, too gaily.[26] Forgetting his note on landlords' servants, Spencer had found it good enough that people received employment from the "middle and upper classes" for producing luxuries for them (S, 292, 210n.). Hole objected, "there is the *small* difference between the laborer taking at once his due share[,] and letting it pass thro the hands of the capitalist, that in the latter case he pays his own labor twice over."[27] Later Spencer acknowledged only that the economic system gave as wages of superintendence too large a share of the total product compared with the share given workers.[28]

Certainly Spencer would have ignored some of Hole's points. Hole asked for state education of unemployed skilled workers.[29] For Spencer, as for Hodgskin and most of their readers, the unemployed (and the underemployed) were either inferiors, or good-for-nothings and vagrants who deserved destitution or jail with hard labor.[30] Hole warned reasonably that repeal of the Poor Law would mean revolt,[31] but not until World War I could it have been proven to Spencer that there really were no unemployables. Hole reminded all Voluntarists opposed to state education, of the record of public education in the United States.[32] This was an example that Spencer had carefully omitted from *Social Statics*.

Finally, both Hodgskin and Spencer could have taken second thought from Hole's sarcasms about their "Nature": "Let the economists' *natural* (or most *un*natural) law of wages, as determined by the fullest competition, be the only recognized one. . . .To depress the laborers' condition . . . by the introduction of Machines, is (with them) quite natural—but to check the operations of these evils, even in the slightest degree, is *artificial*."[33]

Spencer's appeals to nature seem even more incongruous today: "instead of civilization being artificial, it is a part of nature," "natural· causation is displayed among human beings socially aggregated," "the order of Nature existing in the social arrangements of human beings" (S, 60).[34] He never defended, like one laissez-faireist, the low wages of women in factories as the way "Nature effects her own purpose" of keeping mothers at home with their children.[35] Rather, he explained social arrangements by locating human nature as anterior to and separable from social existence.[36] "Human nature," "national character," "the aggregate of men's instincts and sentiments" would become perfectly adapted to social existence through "the slow lapse of generations."[37] The "stern discipline of necessity" would be accomplished by "demand and supply . . . the law of life as well as the law of trade." In the marketplace of life individuals' inherited natures came up against the demands of life in their time and place, and the gains or losses had to be accepted. "Fundamental law, [in] conformity to which life has evolved from its lowest up to its highest forms," required "that each adult individual [should] take the consequences of its own nature and actions: survival of the fittest being the result" (S, 252; E, II, 60). The "unhappy" "transition" to civilization could only be sped up if government did not substitute "artificial" activities for "the natural requirements of the social state" (S, 290).[38]

To those who objected that state intervention no more interfered with competition than the inheritance of wealth did, Spencer could only repeat his assumptions:

> We have to accept, as we may, the established constitution of things, though under it an inferiority for which the individual is not blamable, brings its evils, and a superiority for which he can claim no merit, brings its benefits; and we have to accept, as we may, all those resulting inequalities of advantages which citizens gain by their respective activities. But while it does not devolve upon me to defend the order of Nature, I may say again, . . . that only in virtue of the law under which every creature takes the good and bad results entailed by its inherited organisation, has life advanced to its present height and can continue to advance.[39]

Spencer never considered that his "Nature" was, in effect, an idealization of existing social advantages, which correlated not any more with individual heredity than with the good results that citizens gained. He came to suppose that woman's nature was less highly evolved than man's, would not have her vote, and would not regard marriage as an equal contract.[40] He regretted having supported the Reform Bill of 1867, since "human nature must be much better than it at present is before a much higher civilization can be established."[41] Spencer believed that "the cosmic process" had produced in human society nothing qualitatively different from what biological inheritance had established in other animal species. His commitment to the principle of continuity in all forms of life prevented him from recognizing that people used their capabilities for language to plan and transmit a human, social way of life, a culture, different in kind, not degree, from the life of other social animals. So he supposed that only the survival of individuals fittest for society lessened "the unqualified struggle for existence" among men.[42] Accordingly, he insisted to the last that "competition" of unequals "must persist to the last," and that any interference with such "free play [would] be mischievous."[43] When in 1893, he objected to an American retailer's monopolistic underselling as such an interference, he showed how old-fashioned his economics had become (E, II, 281 - 82). Willy-nilly, competition had led to concentration of capital and to monopolistic practices.

II *The Abstract Individualist*

Spencer's individualism emerges from his conceptions of society, human nature, and government. Since he imagined that man's original life was predatory and antecedent to society (S, 58, 116), he did not conceive what must have been the case—that social relations co-existed with the first stages of human language. So he did not see that social conditions for humans could be different in kind from natural conditions and be alternative stimuli for human development. Instead, each man or woman had to develop his or her biological inheritance. Only the harshest discipline, "to which the animate creation at large is subject," could force men and women through "ages of wearisome application" to acquire intelligence and the ability to work (S, 288, 74).[44] Spencer's view of human possibilities seems a strange one in his age when millions were learning the work discipline of factory labor in one generation.[45] But Spencer's severity about present human nature derived from his austere, religious upbringing; and his individualistic approach to society was normal in his radical political tradition: that of Thomas Paine and Godwin and Hodgskin.[46] There, government was regarded as a *pis aller* for protection and a dangerous meddler with individuals' needs.

Since for Spencer society began when isolated men associated for protection, government would seem to him the major, typifying aspect of any society (S, 227; PS, I, 551). and since he held the Radical view that government was "simply an agent employed in common by a number of individuals to secure them certain advantages," it was easy for Spencer not to be clear that society was always prior to and persisted after any form of government (S, 185).[47] When he said that individuals could ignore the state, he expected them to find nothing but outlawry beyond political combination. Also traditionally, he looked to a distant future, when society would be harmonious and government, unnecessary (S, 193). Then complete civilization would be complete individuality. By the adaptation that humanity was undergoing, one by one, "complete separateness" would finally accompany "perfect mutual dependence" (S, 390 - 91, 396).

Natural rights were the heart of Spencer's political philosophy. He could illustrate social relations and social development by organic analogies, but he never could allow that social organization ever made the general welfare an end in itself. Each individual had a prior claim to happiness (S, 391 - 94, 402 - 08; PS, I, 461-62). Such a stand put Spencer at odds with the Utilitarians, who recognized no natural rights and aimed to calculate the general welfare. Spencer held that the great Jeremy Bentham had contradicted himself in denying natural rights while he maintained the greatest number's right to happiness (S, 27, 87).[48] He also rejected Bentham's view that government could arrange an artificial identity of interests in society. Originally, men grew "unconsciously" into an "associated condition," and therafter only the incalculable, painful adaptation of individuals to natural conditions could advance social life (S, 226).[49] In place of all Utilitarian law-making, Spencer appealed to the moral sense that gave each an intuition of "the liberty of each limited only by the like liberty of all": the "instinct of personal rights" (S, 84, 86). The "reflex function" of this instinct was a sense of justice, or "respect for the claims of others" (S, 90).

Spencer's rephrasing of his rule of political ethics—"Every man has freedom to do all that he wills, provided he infringes not the equal freedom of any other man"—has been immensely attractive to all who would affirm the rights of individuals beyond the moderate position of John Stuart Mill's *On Liberty* (S, 93, 95). The extremity of Spencer's position was also the source of its problems. His standard was a self-sufficient person, who would both spontaneously fulfill his or her nature and incidentally perform the functions of a member of society (S, 225, 251, 397; PS, III, 611).[50] Such an individual would be possible when all others acted as he or she did. The goal for each individual was to do only what he or she would do spontaneously, to be what he or she was naturally (S, 396, 389). The proviso in the rule, then, was relatively incidental. The emphasis was on the individual's liberty, not on his seeing to it that others enjoyed conditions that enabled them to exercise their liberty (E, II, 179). Others had their rights and knew it, or ought to know. Infringement of rights could only be an aggression, a direct blocking of another's desire; neglect, carelessness, or omission could not violate another's liberty to exercise his or her powers (P. 7; S, 185, 295). Even sense of injury was an insufficient test of the limit to liberty. Suffering from one's acts might be beneficial, or the pain and displeasure one inflicted might only result from others' inadequate respect for equal freedom (S, 74, 70).

Spencer felt, nevertheless, that the limit of each person's freedom could almost always be found out exactly (S, 73). But there were difficulties in applying his narrow principle. First, the "claims to equally-limited spheres" were abstract,[51] whereas very concrete in any society was the authority of some to evaluate all claims to share command of others' labor or obedience. In other words, it was disingenuous to speak of equal freedom of opportunity to become more equal than others when the actual choice was whether or not one would seek to gain authority by winning recognition from members of a given social hierarchy. Spencer generalized from his own profession, engineering, that in most occupations, advancement depended "rather on pleasing those in authority than on intrinsic fitness."[52] So equal freedom to enter a trade, a profession, management, or officer training could entail a willingness to block the equal freedom of other entrants to exercise their faculties. From this point of view, at least, Spencer's resistance to public agencies for health, education, and welfare, as well as to state authority in religion and commerce, would be intelligible as a disavowal of state hierarchies.

Second, omission could often seem an infringement of another's equal freedom. Spencer would end Poor Laws at once, even when he could see no feasible way to end landlords' exclusive possession of the soil, to which all men had equal claim.[53] Spencer would declare strikes infractions of consumers' equal freedom, but would not support the public's claims when it misjudged stock promotions (PS, III, 547, 533). As Robert Blatchford asked, could men only object to direct fraud and aggression? Was indirect fraud to be only the hard, and perhaps educative, luck of the buyer?[54]

Third, Spencer's individuals needed to take notice of others only as there were or might be *bona fide* encroachments. Radicalism and Dissent should trouble no one's "philosophic calm," since they were legitimate opponents to authority, which might otherwise become rigid and intolerant of any insubordination.[55] Use of the soil, on the other hand, involved the freedom of all men, so "the consent of society" was necessary (S, 116). Yet how could Spencer's individuals establish sufficient relations with each other to develop social institutions that could grant "consent"? Significantly, Spencer decided that war was the sole initiator of both cooperation and government among primitive people (PS, I, 520; II, 365).[56] Proposing no "theory of the relation of the individual mind to the social system of mind," but only an instinct about mutual encroachments, he could explain subordination and even cooperation only as results of aggression.[57]

One may ask whether in recommending each man's equal freedom to exercise his faculties, Spencer had an adequate estimate of people's capabilities. He conceived of people as originally and by nature separate individuals. But people have exercised their faculties not only separately, like mental workers alone with a language, but also cooperatively, like manual workers combining their labor on a project. Spencer, the "brain worker," underestimated the socializing effects of cooperative manual work (PS, III, 569). His supposition that people could only be forced to cooperate by war, and to work by "the severest discipline," suffering, reflected his lack of experience of social labor. Cooperation as certainly began with social labor, like hunting, as government did with war. Although he was impressed by the division of labor, Spencer emphasized not cooperation, but the advantage of specialization to the individual, as "a line of least resistance" (PS, III, 342, 359). He saw the highest form of combined labor in "entirely voluntary" piecework in a workers' cooperative (PS, III, 572). As a result, there was very little content both to his "elaborate form of mutual dependence" and to his "complete individuality" (S, 396, 390).[58] The dependence was only incidental, a platform; and the individuality would not become an end in itself until wars and commercial struggle had "used up [countless generations] for the benefit of posterity" (PS, III, 525) Spencer's individualism could seem self-evident only to a reader who did not see how unreally isolated Spencer's individual was and how low an opinion Spencer had of the faculties that most people have increasingly exercised in social labor.

III *State*

Spencer distrusted government for two reasons. First, he saw Parliament as a center of "class power" for "the landed interest," which it served by "class legislation" (S, 197).[59] In this respect, he made use of the Radical tactic of pointing to the great majority in the House of Commons of landowners, army and navy officers, and lawyers. In a government so dominated by persons with whom considerations of rank and inheritance were foremost, rigidity and inefficiency would result (PS, II, 254, 260, 357; E, II, 231). Second, he saw the English government as trying to do the impossible: calculate the happiness of millions. This was doing the wrong thing for the wrong reason. People had to take the consequences of their natures and actions. And happiness was not calculable, but was a result; it would be the end of the line of least resistance followed by supply and demand, which was analogous to the survival of the fittest.

Spencer's first reason for distrust was not conclusive, and he did not take it so even while he lost touch with contemporary politics. During his lifetime, the English government continued to be dominated by representatives of the land-owning upper class. Yet he continued to support representative government as the most advanced arrangement possible in his time.[60] And he continued to react to Liberal-Conservative politics like a middle-class Radical of 1850. In *Social Statics,* he had exposed ruling class unity: "Some thousands of individuals having identical interests, moving together in the same circle, brought up with like prejudices, educated in one creed, bound together by family ties, and meeting annually in the same city may easily enough combine for the obtainment of a desired object" (S, 198; PS, II, 409). In 1854 he had noted the interest of landowners in railways; but he never realized—as Dickens did, in depicting the Barnacle family's interest in the financier Merdle—the extent of upper class support for new heavy industry and for the export of capital to South Africa and India.[61]

Rigid in his political preconceptions, Spencer missed the shuffle of left and right after 1850. In 1851 he had doubted, from the example of Chartism, that twelve million workingmen, even if they had votes and wished to do so, could ever unite to infringe upon the rights of "the rich hundreds." In 1891 he had become certain that the working classes would use their votes to break the law of equal freedom by taking earnings from "the superior" to supplement the earnings of "the less diligent or the less capable." So then he favored representation in Commons not of individuals, but of interests (E, II, 192). But Parliament already represented interests, not individuals, when Spencer rose up in 1881 - 82 to organize the Anti-Aggression League against English imperialism in Egypt. Yet he reverted to his view of 1842 that the government was listening only to "the organs of the upper classes," pursuing a policy of increasing armaments and so multiplying places for younger sons.[62] He saw English imperialism as "abominable filibustering" and "political burglaries."[63] He could not recognize it as a stage in the evolution of capitalism, though he could see that it suited the majority of the population.[64] Since the principles of political economy explained "the normal relations of industrial actions," he expected no evolution, but only abnormality, "pathological states," beyond those principles.[65] To him, the nation seemed headed for "rebarbarization"; and Liberalism seemed to have become the "new Toryism," for its regulation of commerce and establishment of national primary education.[66] He never understood that whereas reduction of government jurisdiction, which had been a Radical proposal in 1850, had been taken up by the new Conservatives, welfare programs, once associated with Tory defenders of a Poor Law, had become a new Liberal concern.[67]

Spencer's second reason for distrusting the government also was not conclusive. If society had its science, but men dared not apply its principles to society, then how was it that they applied physics in engineering?[68] If individuals could learn from their experience, however slowly, how was it that individuals in government could not also learn by practice?[69] If bureaucrats were prone to rationalize their mistakes as having been made for the right reasons, Spencer rationalized that although the morals of trade were "commercial cannibalism," businessmen's only mistake was to respect wealth rather than the "mental power" that it signified.[70] It might be, after all, that progress would not be increased activity in separateness, as Spencer thought, but more and more practice by associations of citizens and by government agencies at reducing the misery of millions.[71]

Spencer was inconsistent, in any case, in his belief in reserving the administration of justice for the government. As James Hole pointed out, any argument against other governmental interventions was also valid against this one.[72] Spencer wanted government to defend the poor against aggressions by the rich; to administer civil, as well as criminal justice free of charge; and to provide quick, certain, and free remedies for breaches of contract.[73] He also specified supervision against pollution of the air and for new uses of land and water (E, II, 212, 83). He wanted government to specialize as an umpire of the law of equal freedom. But if the officers of the courts were members of the propertied class (PS, II, 512), what could prevent continuance of inequalities like those of the Master and Servant Act of 1823? Under it, employers were subject only to civil action (at the worker's expense) for recovery of wages, whereas workers were subject to criminal action (at no expense to the employer) for absence or disobedience, and faced as penalties loss of wages, imprisonment, and return to work for the employer.[74] Spencer could recognize and resist authority in religious and political hierarchies, but felt no discomfort with the authority, the "mental power," of wealth.[75] He probably supposed that through generations of exercise in the courts in the law of equal freedom, individuals would acquire a strong sentiment for justice and to that extent assimilate.[76]

Spencer called his restriction of government to justice and national defense "specialized administration." He compared an industrial society so governed and not at war to the viscera of a higher animal. The unregulated economy would function spontaneously, like a digestive system. The sympathetic and vasomotor nervous systems would involuntarily prompt the supply of more blood if there was more digestive activity, just as the marketplace could share out returns without central control, providing that the government administered justice. As the brain (mind) only restrained the stomach (appetite), so the government only maintained order and regulated contracts so that equal freedom brought its benefits and penalties for more or less fit competitive activity.[77] Now, it is noticeable that when Spencer compared the society that he would prefer to a deracinated organism, he revealed his low estimate of people's capability, intelligence, and experience in government. In other places, he compared government to the regulating organs—the cerebro-muscular system—of a higher animal. This system had charge of the outer activity, including any cooperative work, done by the organism (PS, I, 548). Because he would deny that people ought to work in central political institutions to plan and coordinate many of the activities of society, Spencer was willing to adopt a nonsensical analogy. He neglected to explain how his alimentary society would get its food and how raw materials and unfinished goods would enter its economy. In the last century, governments of industrial societies have shared with corporations the direction of investment and trade, to secure food, raw materials, and unfinished goods from pre-industrial societies.

Spencer probably got his organic analogy from the columns of *The Economist*, and perhaps he saw the current schoolbook analogy of the rich man to the stomach.[78] Since he thought much of his analogy, it is strange that he could falsify it by comparing the kind of society he preferred, a voluntaristic industrial society, to a lower, automatic organism. That allowed the caste-dominated militant society, which he felt was less civilized, to stand analogous to higher, conscious animals.[79] He could stand for this, nevertheless, since he was committed to laissez-faire notions of society and government. He did not perceive how important government had become for the development of the new 'free trade' of exporting capital and for the military defense of colonies. It is to his credit as an individual that he would not accept and tried to stop his government's "political burglaries" overseas; but his resistance to what was, did not enable him to understand it. Indeed, his recommendations for politics, in general, suggest Richard Potter's comment at the end of a cheerful argument with his friend: "Won't work, Spencer; won't work, my dear fellow."[80]

Spencer's economics and political philosophy can seem wrongheaded a century later. But by treating supply and demand and the survival of the fittest analogously, as laws both of life and of society, he encouraged people to accept social inequalities.[81] The wide acceptability of his analogies derived from the fresh support they could give to existing ideology for social subordination. Most of his first readers were probably more narrow-minded than he about the natural rights of property owners and the idle disposition of any unemployed person.[82] As industrial society became more hierarchical and authoritarian after 1890, Spencer's views ironically continued to seem apt despite his anti-Establishment and anti-imperialist politics. The analogies he had used to defend individualism and self-regulation were adopted as "natural" laws to justify rationalization in business organization and efficiency in work.[83] He had counselled that if each individual took upon himself the consequences of his or her nature and actions within the division of labor, the benefit for future individuals would be slow social progress. So, rationalizers in industrial societies found prescription in Spencer for some persons to use others for future benefits.

CHAPTER 9

Audience and Influence

CERTAINLY a million copies of Spencer's books were sold.[1] He spent the equivalent of $200,000 today in publishing his philosophy, and especially the *Descriptive Sociology*. But he shrewdly limited his English publishers to a ten percent commission. As a result, he enjoyed an "ample" income from 1869 until his death.[2] He left an estate equivalent to nearly $400,000 today, for the express purpose of continuing publication of the *Descriptive Sociology*.[3]

From Spencer's collection of translations of his works, it is clear that there was world-wide interest in his thought during the last quarter of the nineteenth century. First in France and Russia, in 1866, and then in Germany, Italy, and Spain during the 1870's and 1880's, "The Classification of Sciences," *First Principles*, and *Education* were translators' early choices. With the exception of the sociology, which was in progress, all of the major works were available in Germany and Russia by 1876.[4] Thirty-two Japanese translations appeared from 1877 to 1900, and there were Chinese translations of *The Study of Sociology* and the sociology in 1903 and 1908.[5] These translations did not reflect popular interest only. From 1876 to 1897, Spencer received (and tried to decline) honors from eighteen learned societies in Italy, France, the United States, Denmark, Belgium, Greece, Austria, Hungary, and Russia.[6]

I *Politics*

Spencer's thought proved to be most useful to some political conservatives in England, the United States, Mexico, and Japan. In *Physics and Politics* (1869), Walter Bagehot shared Spencer's (and Carlyle's) low estimate of prehistoric man, quoted Spencer on population, and referred to him on heredity and adaptation.[7] Bagehot did not live to see Spencer's full denigration of the militant society, which he himself defended without compunction.[8] On Spencer's suggestion that Satan might show heaven that contemporary man was more wicked than the devil, Little Englander Wilfrid Scawen Blunt wrote a long poem against the hypocrisies of the Christian British Empire. In *Satan Absolved* (1899), the Angel of Pity confirmed the devil's testimony that the White Man had ruined the world for "the burden of his cash." Except that he foresaw "a remote future of a desirable kind," Spencer said that he would accept "the sweeping away of the whole race"; and he thought that Blunt's poem "ought to bring to their senses millions of hypocrites who profess[ed] the current religion."[9]

In the United States, Spencer's notion of social justice—that each adult should accept the consequences of his nature and actions according to supply and demand—found extraordinary acceptance within the dominant Republican Party.[10] Wealthy Americans honored Spencer at dinner at Delmonico's on November 9, 1882. Carl Schurz recalled having read *Social Statics* in camp during the Civil War; and Henry Ward Beecher declared that Spencer's truth, including the view that people could not be protected from the results of their own follies, "had been meat and drink to him for twenty years."[11] Spencer told his hosts that he did not admire the big business man who became enslaved to accumulation and took an immoderate share of an industry or profession. He had a high regard, however, for his later admirer, Andrew Carnegie.[12] Three Justices of the Supreme Court were avowed Spencerians and participated in decisions recognizing corporations as individuals, and disallowing government regulation of contracts with regard to hours of work, a minimum wage, or child labor.[13] In 1905, Justice Oliver Wendell Holmes reminded his colleagues that "the Fourteenth Amendment does not enact Mr. Herbert Spencer's *Social Statics*."[14]

In Mexico, supporters of dictator Porfirio Diaz used Spencer's terms to argue for the need for order before heterogeneity could develop.[15] In 1873, the Japanese Ambassador to the United States, Mori Arinori, sought Spencer's advice about a draft for a constitution for his country. The framers of the 1890 constitution, Baron Kaneko and Count Ito, also studied Spencer and asked his advice in 1892 about relations with the West.[16] He counselled little departure from existing social arrangements—despotic rule and patriarchal kinship systems—since social change could only occur slowly, by adaptation. He also warned against allowing foreign settlements, as leading to eventual subjugation, and against inter-marriage with foreigners, as invariably bringing bad biological results.

Some socialists and liberals found use for aspects of Spencer's thought. Henry George used the Persistence of Force and Spencer's population theory to argue against Malthus.[17] European socialists could cite Spencer on the survival of the fittest in support of class struggle, and anarchist Emma Goldman regarded Spencer's law of equal freedom as most important.[18] In Czarist Russia, populist Nicholas Mikhailovsky admired "On Manners and Fashion" and "Progress: Its Law and Cause." Adopting Spencer's antagonism to the prestige of customs, he reversed Spencer's emphasis on the division of labor and defined progress as the heterogeneity of the individual personality, rather than of social production.[19] In Japan, liberals used *Social Statics,* while conservatives studied Spencer the sociologist. Meanwhile in China, Yen Fu found a programme for nationalism in Spencer's model of the social organism. He could also uphold Spencer''s emphasis on egoism against the Confucian condemnation of self-interest, since he believed that in the concept of the Unknowable Spencer saw the cosmos like a Chinese mystic.[20] The heroes of the Chinese Revolution, Mao Tse-tung and Lu Hsun, read Spencer before they came to Marx and Lenin.[21]

II *Literature*

Besides those interested in nineteenth-century evolutionary thought, or in conservative thought, or in the special topics of Chapters 4 though 8, students of literature from 1860 to 1920 might well read Spencer today. At least twelve authors in England, the United States, France, and Russia both read at least *First Principles* and made use of Spencer's ideas in their fictions. In England, George Eliot, Thomas Hardy, Olive Schreiner, Arnold Bennett, D. H. Lawrence, and Aldous Huxley alluded to Spencer.[22] There is room here for only a few examples, chosen from the last three novelists.

Arnold Bennett read *First Principles* through the winter of 1906 - 07 (on his honeymoon) before he began his masterpiece, *The Old Wives' Tale*. Applying the universal postulate rather than learning, Bennett rated Spencer as the supreme philosopher:

> Tonight I finished *First Principles*. I suppose I can never have again the same thrills of admiration as this book has given me. If any book could be called the greatest book in the world, I suppose this can. I have never read anything a tenth part so comprehensive. And it makes its effects by sheer

honest argumentative force. There are no ornaments of brilliance, wit, ingenuity, or even eloquence. Yet the closing pages of Part I, and the closing pages of Part II, are equally overwhelming in their effect. Faults there, of course, are in it but it is surely the greatest achievement of any human mind. This I do think. And Spencer has not yet come into his own, in England. As a *philosopher*, in the real sense—not as a discoverer, or a man of science—but as a philosopher, he is supreme in the history of intelligence. I say this, not because I have read all the other great ones, but because I cannot imagine the possibility of anyone having produced anything else as great as *First Principles*.[23]

Bennett's nineteen realistic novels show the influence of Spencer on characterization, imagery, and vocabulary.

D. H. Lawrence had Miriam Leivers read Spencer and think that Paul Morel took "the bitterness of life badly"—the trap "baited with the guts of a rabbit," "the weasel with its teeth in a rabbit's throat," the survival of the fittest. But at the end she "crouched" while he "escap[ed] like a weasel out of her hands."[24]

In "Uncle Spencer," T. H. Huxley's grandson gave an amusing account of an eccentric Victorian autodidact whose theories left him unable to adapt when caught in the 1914 German invasion through Belgium. He held to an "obsoletely mechanistic" physiology and argued that modern men had descended from African pigmies.[25] Spencer had conceived of organisms mechanistically and had believed that the necks of giraffes had lengthened through use-inheritance. So Huxley's uncle was well named: pigmies' legs could lengthen, too. After World War I, Uncle Spencer's nephew, the teller of the tale, tried to guard against being like his uncle: "too promptly logical to draw conclusions from false premises."[26] Like Uncle Spencer, the philosopher had not allowed for "the passive malignity of matter"—the second law of thermodynamics—and for "the stupidity or duplicity of man"—any person's indefinite number of roles.[27]

In the United States, Lafcadio Hearn, Hamlin Garland, Theodore Dreiser, and Jack London were strongly affected by their readings in Spencer.[28] The one who made Spencer most important for a character was London, for his Martin Eden. London read Spencer "to get a basic knowledge for writing"; Eden found from *First Principles* that all was law, regarded Spencer as the father of psychology, found his autobiography as full of romance as any thrilling novel, and attacked his academic detractors.[29]

In France, Jules Laforgue, and in Russia, Leo Tolstoy and Anton

Chekhov took Spencer seriously.[30] In Tolstoy's *The Resurrection* (1899), the landowner Nekhludov realized "all the cruelty and injustice of private ownership of land" from reading Chapter IX of *Social Statics*.[31] In "The Duel" (1891), Chekhov presented a representative Spencerian in von Koren, who said, "I'm a zoologist, or a sociologist, which is one and the same." Like Spencer, von Koren was independent and stubborn, studied the development of jellyfish, and advocated "annihilation of the feeble and worthless."[32]

III *Conclusion*

In his own era of great economic and ideological changes, Herbert Spencer yoked the old with the new and won an enormous, international reputation. His supreme self-confidence saw him through the construction of a system of philosophy and won him the liking and help of men and women who respected his egoism. He impressed thousands by his ease in expounding scientific theories by the familiar concepts of force and use-inheritance. He awed thousands more by ranging under his definition of evolution not only the nebular hypothesis, the conservation of energy, and natural selection, but also laissez-faire economics, political individualism, and a utilitarian ethic. He won minds by the calm, poised sentences by which he enunciated the evolution of all aggregates by the reactions of their units to external influences. When he died in 1903, he was both the most famous and the most popular philosopher of his age. Many still saw him as a second Newton.

For many reasons, Spencer's reputation has remained exceedingly low during most of the twentieth century. Not training himself to observe what was adequate evidence in any field of natural science, he relied on what he had learned—mechanics and classification—to explain the dynamics of the evolution of mind and of inorganic and organic matter. Heroically aiming to unify the sciences by a theory of development, in effect he speculated how nearly they might be reduced to Newtonian physics. Expounding 'super-organic' evolution, he too often referred it to aggregates of biological units, and never realized the key importance of the capacity for language in the establishment and transmission of human culture. Refusing to read an author with whom he could not agree, he claimed solutions in epistemology and metaphysics when he had oversimplified the problems. Convinced before the age of thirty that he knew the natural laws of economics, politics, and ethics, he could never criticize his concepts of economic and ethical value. But in the last quarter of the twentieth century, when the errors in Spencer's procedures and tenets have become unmistakable, readers of various interests might once again consult Spencer according to their needs.

To the growing nineteenth-century collection of uniform, self-acting laws of nature, Spencer added two that he gave special emphasis to. He contributed a law justifying the competition of unequals (the law of equal freedom) and a law guaranteeing slow progress and rationalizing hierarchical division of labor in both physiology and society (use-inheritance). He worked out these laws in his psychology, ethics, biology, sociology, and politics. He was especially ingenious in his psychology and biology. In the former, he correlated the conscious moves of the mind with the unconscious actions of the nerves and extended learning by association from the individual's experience to the experience of the species. In the latter, he was more philosophical and could seem more precise than Darwin. He related biological development to a definition of universal evolution, and he offered mechanistic explanations at almost every stage in his biology. His phrase for natural selection, "the survival of the fittest," seemed as clear as Spencer's Law on the relations of surface to volume and of size and weight to fecundity. All in all, his encyclopedic system is still amazing.

Notes and References

Chapter One

1. Eric Robinson, "The Derby Philosophical Society," *Annals of Science*, 9 (1953), 359 - 67.

2. Lillie B. Lamar, "Herbert Spencer and His Father," *University of Texas Studies in English*, 32 (1953), 59 - 66. Spencer also did not acknowledge parallels to works by Joseph Priestley, on the worth of science, and by Claude Marcel, on teaching modern languages: H. G. Good, "The Sources of Spencer's *Education*," *Journal of Educational Research*, 13 (1926), 325 - 35; Norman T. Walker, "The Sources of Herbert Spencer's Educational Ideas," *ibid.*, 22 (1930), 299 - 308.

3. *An Autobiography* (New York, 1904), I, 140. Volume and page references to this title appear in the text of this chapter. Spencer advocated a generous nutrition and warm clothing, rather than the fashionable, "hardening" diets and cold bedrooms: J. A. Banks, *Prosperity and Parenthood* (London, 1954), pp. 170 - 72.

4. David Duncan, *The Life and Letters of Herbert Spencer* (London, 1908), p. 56. In the text of this chapter, page references to this title appear with the letter "D."

5. *The Later Letters of John Stuart Mill, 1849 - 73*, ed. Francis E. Mineka and Dwight N. Lindley, *Collected Works* (Toronto, 1972), XV, 1210.

6. *The Principles of Ethics* (New York, 1898), I, 50.

7. For a Freudian analysis of Spencer, see Richard L. Schoenwald's "Town Guano and 'Social Statics,' " *Victorian Studies*, 11 (1968), 707 - 10.

8. "The Function of Criticism at the Present Time" (1864), *Lectures and Essays in Criticism*, in *Complete Prose Works*, ed. R. H. Super (Ann Arbor, Mich., 1962), III, 267.

9. "Personal Reminiscences of Herbert Spencer," *Forum*, 35 (1904), 615.

10. G. H. Hardy, *A Mathematicians's Apology* (Cambridge, 1948), p. 28.

11. Josiah Royce, *Herbert Spencer* (New York, 1904), p. 181.

12. Knowles (1798 - 1817) had titled the poem "The Three Tabernacles," but it is known as "Lines Written in the Churchyard of Richmond, Yorkshire."

13. *Herbert Spencer* (New York, 1971), Chapters 1 - 3.

14. *The Proper Sphere of Government* (London, 1843), p. 5.

15. William Paley, *The Principles of Moral and Political Philosophy* (1785) (Cambridge, Mass., 1830), p. 40.

16. *The Proper Sphere of Government,* p. 13.
17. *Proper Sphere,* pp. 13, 35.
18. *Proper Sphere,* pp. 37, 39.
19. R.S. Neale, "Class and Ideology in a Provincial City: Bath 1800 - 1850," in *Class and Ideology in the Nineteenth Century* (London, 1972), pp. 57 - 58.
20. Elie Halévy, *Victorian Years, 1841 - 1895* (1946), in *A History of the English People in the Nineteenth Century* (New York, 1961), IV, 35n.
21. Alexander Wilson, "The Suffrage Movement," in *Pressure from Without in Early Victorian England,* ed. Patricia Hollis (London, 1974), pp. 86 - 91.
22. Thomas Cooper, *The Life of Thomas Cooper Written by Himself* (London, 1876), p. 224q.
23. Charles M. Elliott, "The Ideology of Economic Growth: A Case Study," in *Land, Labour and Population in the Industrial Revolution,* ed. E. L. Jones and G. E. Mingay (New York, 1967), pp. 90 - 94.
24. *The Proper Sphere of Government,* p. 25. *Social Statics* (1851) (New York, 1954), p. 69.
25. *Social Statics.* p. 316.
26. *Social Statics,* pp. 288, 315, 338.
27. *Social Statics,* p. 291.
28. *Social Statics,* p. 289.
29. *Social Statics,* pp. 315 - 16. *The Proper Sphere of Government,* p. 13.
30. Elsa Peverly Kimball, *Sociology and Education: An Analysis of the Theories of Spencer and Ward* (1932) (New York, 1968), p. 149.
31. *Social Statics,* p. 339.
32. Q. Joseph D. Hooker, in John Fiske, *Edward Livingston Youmans* (New York, 1894), p. 283; Grant Allan, "Personal Reminiscences," 614; "Michael Field" [Edith Cooper], *Works and Days* (London, 1933), pp. 131 - 33.
33. Mrs. Lynn Linton was caricatured in the press as Mrs. Grundy: F. B. Smith, *Radical Artisan* (Totowa, N.J., 1973), p. 164.
34. Eliot wrote of her "calm *new* friendship": *The George Eliot Letters,* ed. Gordon S. Haight (New Haven, 1954 - 55), II, 29.
35. Peel, *Herbert Spencer,* pp. 37, 273n.
36. "Address to Working Men, by Felix Holt" (1868), in *Essays of George Eliot,* ed. Thomas Pinney (New York, 1963), p. 426.
37. *Little Dorrit* (1857), Chapter 10.
38. Richard L. Schoenwald, " 'George Eliot's "Love" Letters': Unpublished Letters from George Eliot to Herbert Spencer," *Bulletin of the New York Public Library,* 79 (1976), 369 - 70.
39. *The George Eliot Letters,* VI, 124; IV, 489.
40. The obstacle would not have been that Spencer knew the secret that she had been in love with John Chapman: Gordon S. Haight, *George Eliot and John Chapman* (New Haven, 1940), pp. 21 - 22, 32.

41. *The Study of Sociology* (1873) (Ann Arbor, Mich., 1961), p. 343. Eliot read *Social Statics* three times and *The Data of Ethics* twice: *An Autobiography,* II, p. 428.

42. Roy M. MacLeod, "The X-Club: A Social Network of Science in Late-Victorian England," *Notes and Records of Royal Society of London,* 24 (1970), 308.

43. MacLeod, pp. 310 - 11, 321n.

44. "The Belfast Address," in *Fragments of Science* (New York, 1897), II, 185. Not everyone liked Spencer. Carlyle called him an "immeasurable ass": Duncan, p. 378q., cf. *An Autobiography,* I, 440 - 44. Canon Barnett and his wife, with whom Spencer toured Egypt, found him "a Casaubon" and a bore: Henrietta Octavia Barnett, *Canon Barnett* (London, 1918), I, 238, 241.

45. Huxley, Tyndall, and Spencer were the Committee; Tyndall, Spencer, and Lubbock were the contributors.

46. Attendance at the largest meetings of scientists averaged no more that 2100 during the nineteenth century, although 3838 met in Manchester in 1887. O. J. R. Howarth, *The British Association for the Advancement of Science: A Retrospect, 1831 - 1931* (London, 1931), pp. 117 - 19. There were still only 5000 scientists in England in 1911, but 49,000 in 1951: John Burnett, *A History of the Cost of Living* (Harmondsworth, England, 1969), p. 295.

47. Spencer declined candidacies for professorships at London and Edinburgh, and nominations to university rectorships at St. Andrews, Edinburgh, and Aberdeen: Duncan, pp. 588 - 89; *An Autobiography,* II, 172. *First Principles* and *The Principles of Biology* were textbooks at Oxford in 1869. William James lectured on *The Principles of Psychology* at Harvard in 1876, and William Graham Sumner defended *The Study of Sociology* at Yale in 1879. Cf. *An Autobiography,* II, 242 - 43; Richard Hofstadter, *Social Darwinism in American Thought* (1944) (Boston, 1955), p. 20.

48. His forthcoming book, *Nature's Place in Man,* will tell the full story. On Victorian scientific naturalism, see Frank Miller Turner, *Between Science and Religion* (New Haven, 1974), pp. 17 - 30, 142.

49. J. Vernon Jenson, "The X Club: Fraternity of Victorian Scientists," *British Journal for the History of Science,* 5 (1970). 63.

50. Charles Coulston Gillispie, *Genesis and Geology* (Cambridge, Mass., 1951). Robert Young, "The Historiographic and Ideological Contexts of the Nineteenth-Century Debate on Man's Place in Nature," in *Changing Perspectives in the History of Science,* ed. Mukulás Teich and Robert Young (London, 1973), p. 372q. Peter J. Bowler, *Fossils and Progress* (New York, 1976).

51. Brian Inglis, *Poverty and the Industrial Revolution* (London, 1972), pp. 101, 434 - 36, 458. Elie Halévy, *The Growth of Philosophic Radicalism,* tr. Mary Morris (Boston, 1955), p. 489.

52. Young, in Teich, p. 403. Young, "Evolutionary Biology and

Ideology: Then and Now," *Science Studies,* 1 (1971), 202.

53. J. W. Burrow, *Evolution and Society* (Cambridge, 1966), pp. 211 - 12.

54. Grant Allen, science teacher and writer, wrote, "Thy voice first told us man was nature's child, / And in one common law proclaimed them reconciled": "To Herbert Spencer," *The Lower Slopes* (London, 1894), p. 45.

55. *The Principles of Ethics,* I, 190q.

56. James F. Rodgers, "The Physical Spencer, I, II," *Scientific Monthly,* 11, 12 (June, July 1920), 570 - 80, 53 - 65.

57. John H. Winslow has shown the possibilities that Darwin was poisoned by prescriptions: *Darwin's Victorian Malady* (Philadelphia, 1971), pp. 28 - 30, 31, 34, 87n. For Spencer's symptoms, compare, *ibid.*, pp. 65, 67, 67 - 70, 72.

58. Beatrice Potter Webb observed that he was a great taker of morphine: *My Apprenticeship* (New York, 1926), p. 36.

59. *Social Statics,* pp. 338 - 39.

60. Walter Troughton said that whenever the barometer fell, the unarthritic Spencer expected to feel wretched. He would stop his cab to feel his pulse; and when one day he fell down the double staircase at the Athenaeum Club, he jumped up unhurt and felt his pulse: "Reminisciences," MS, Athenaeum Club Library; see T. D. Rodgers, "Handlist of the Herbert Spencer Papers (MS 791) deposited in the University of London Library by the Athenaeum," University of London, 1972.

61. For coincidences, see *An Autobiography,* I, 384, 527; II, 425.

62. Isaac Bashevis Singer, "The Spinoza of Market Street," in *The Spinoza of Market Street* (New York, 1958), pp. 23 - 24.

Chapter Two

1. *An Autobiography* (New York, 1904), II, 527.

2. *Mark Twain - Howells Letters,* ed. Henry Nash Smith and William M. Gibson (Cambridge, Mass, 1960), I, 419. "On Style," in *The Handling of Words* (1923), ed. Royal A. Gettmann (Lincoln, Neb., 1968), p. 39.

3. "Personal Reminiscences of Herbert Spencer," *Forum,* 35 (April - June 1904), 616.

4. *An Autobiography,* II, 527 - 28; cf. I, 182.

5. "Letter VII," p. 27. The findings from this text and from four other titles by Spencer, as well as from texts by T. B. Macaulay, Matthew Arnold, and T. H. Huxley, are available from the author. The four Spencer texts are in *Social Statics, Education, The Study of Sociology,* and *The Principles of Sociology.*

6. Dwight Bolinger, "Maneuvering for Stress and Intonation" (1957), in *Forms of English* (Cambridge, Mass., 1965), pp. 309 - 15.

7. *An Autobiography,* II, 40, 42q. ("diffuse"). The sentence quoted: (1873) (Ann Arbor, Mich., 1961), p. 204. The "notion" was Matthew Arnold's that "we are backward in appreciating and pursuing abstract

knowledge," q. in *The Study of Sociology*, p. 197, from the London *Times*, 1873.

8. "Herbert Spencer," *Le Temps* (11 December 1903), p. 1.

9. *An Autobiography*, I, 181, 264. George Bion Denton showed that "Force of Expression" (1843 - 44) must have supplied the substance for all but the last paragraph of the later essay: "Origin and Development of Herbert Spencer's Principle of Economy," in *The Fred Newton Scott Anniversary Papers* (1929) (Freeport, N.Y., 1968), pp. 55 - 92.

10. *An Autobiography*, I, 408, cf. 362. "The Philosophy of Style," *Essays* (New York, 1899), II, 366. Page references in this chapter are to this essay. George Bion Denton, "Herbert Spencer and the Rhetoricians," *PMLA*, 34 (1919), 89 - 111.

11. Travis R. Merritt, "Taste, Opinion, and Theory in the Rise of Victorian Prose Stylism," in *The Art of Victorian Prose*, ed. George Levine and William Madden (New York, 1968), pp. 15 - 19.

12. *The Proper Sphere of Government*, "Letter VIII," p. 28.

13. "What Knowledge is of most Worth?" (1859), in *Education* (1861) (London, 1911), pp. 34 - 35; *The Principles of Psychology* (New York, 1899), I, 327, 485.

14. See Fred W. Householder, Jr., and Roman Jakobson on literary language, in *Style in Language*, ed. Thomas A. Sebeok (Cambridge, Mass., 1960), pp. 341ff., and 371, 377, resp.

15. "What Knowledge is of most Worth?" p. 37.

16. *The Study of Sociology*, p. 367.

Chapter Three

1. J. Arthur Thomson, *Herbert Spencer* (London, 1906), p. 212. William James, "Herbert Spencer's Autobiography," in *Memories and Studies* (London, 1911), p. 126.

2. "On the Advisableness of Improving Natural Knowledge" (1866) in *Methods and Results, Collected Essays* (1893) (Hildesheim, 1970), I, 38.

3. *Social Statics* (1851) (New York, 1954), pp. 424 - 25. *Essays* (New York, 1899), I, 62 - 63. *First Principles*, Fourth Edition (New York, 1958), pp. 133, 548. Page references in this chapter are to this edition. *The Principles of Sociology* (New York, 1899), III, 173 - 75.

4. *The George Eliot Letters*, ed. Gordon S. Haight (New Haven, 1954 - 55), II, 341. Eliot said that there was "more feeling in it than we generally get in his writing." Bennett, *The Journals*, ed. Frank Swinnerton (Harmondsworth, England, 1971) p. 219. Webb, *My Apprenticeship* (New York, 1926), pp. 93 - 94.

5. *First Principles*, pp. 53 - 56, 88 - 90, q. Mansel, *Limits of Religious Thought* (1859), pp. 85 - 87, q. Sir William Hamilton's "On the Philosophy of the Unconditioned," *Discussions on Philosophy and Literature* (London, 1853), pp. 1 - 38.

6. One instance was the simultaneous inconceivability and necessity of

the hypothesis of a universal ether as a medium through which gravitation might work: *First Principles,* pp. 72 - 73, 114.

7. The difficulties with Spencer's account of force and consciousness will be indicated in Chapter 4.

8. *An Autobiography* (New York, 1904), I, 397.

9. *Essays,* I, 62 - 63.

10. *Essays,* I, 109, 155, 129.

11. "The Unknowable" (Oxford, 1923), p. 18. Santayana, *Skepticism and Animal Faith* (1923) (New York, 1955), pp. 99 - 108.

12. "Mr. Spencer's Psychological Congruities, II," *Mind,* 6 (1881), 406.

13. He also used many other terms, such as "Unconditioned Cause" and "Creative Power": *First Principles,* pp. 175, 120.

14. William Torrey Harris, "Herbert Spencer," *Journal of Speculative Philosophy,* 1 (1867), p. 15. "Replies to Criticisms," *Essays,* II, p. 251. James Iverach, "Herbert Spencer," *The Critical Review of Theological and Philosophical Literature,* 14 (1904), pp. 106 - 07.

15. Malcolm Guthrie, *On Mr. Spencer's Formula of Evolution* (London, 1879), p. 163. Also, *On Mr. Spencer's Unification of Knowledge* (London, 1882), p. 127.

16. Leo Tolstoy, *Anna Karenina,* tr. Constance Garnett, ed. L. J. Kent and N. Berberova (New York, 1965), p. 835.

17. *The Principles of Psychology* (New York, 1899), I, 145, 636 - 40q.

18. *Principles of Psychology,* II, 593q.

19. *The Canon of Reason and Virtue, being Lao-tze's Tao Tĕn King,* tr., ed. Paul Carus (La Salle, Ill., 1913, 1954), pp. 73 - 74q., 131 - 32, 146 - 47. See Benjamin Schwartz, *In Search of Wealth and Power: Yen Fu and the West* (Cambridge, Mass., 1964), pp. 53, 199. The deepest religious consciousness to Spencer was one "which transcends the forms of distinct thought": *The Principles of Sociology,* III, 169.

20. William B. Carpenter, *Principles of Physiology, General and Comparative* (1839), Third Edition (1851). On von Baer and Carpenter, Jane Oppenheimer, "An Embryological Enigma in the 'Origin of Species,'" in *Forerunners of Darwin, 1745 - 1859,* ed. Bentley Glass et al. (1959) (Baltimore, 1968), pp. 309 - 11. *An Autobiography* (New York, 1904), I, 470, II, 9. David Duncan, *The Life and Letters of Herbert Spencer* (London, 1908), p. 546. *First Principles,* pp. 336 - 37n.

21. *An Autobiography,* I, 538, II, 195 - 96.

22. *Essays,* I, 9, 37 - 38.

23. *Essays,* I, 92, 102. Duncan, p. 549.

24. *Essays,* I, 10 - 11, 60.

25. The Bridgewater Treatises and William Whewell's works had prepared the Victorians to see continuity in natural phenomena: Walter F. Cannon, "The Problem of Miracles in the 1830's," *Victorian Studies,* 4 (1960), 5 - 32. See also Peter J. Bowler, *Fossils and Progress* (New York, 1976), pp. 54 - 55, 72 - 73. John Theodore Merz said that English natural theology "really culminated in Herbert Spencer": *A History of European*

Thought in the Nineteenth Century (1903), Third Edition (Edinburgh, 1928), II, 323n.

26. *An Autobiography,* II, 14 - 15q. Duncan, p. 550. Spencer had adopted "evolution" as a word free of the anthropomorphic meaning of "progress": *ibid.*, p. 551n. He knew William R. Grove's *The Correlation of Physical Forces* (1843). In E. L. Youmans, ed., *The Correlation and Conservation of Forces* (New York, 1865). Peter J. Bowler, "The Changing Meaning of Evolution," *Journal of the History of Ideas,* 76(1975), 109.

27. *An Autobiography,* II, 16 - 19. Duncan, pp. 426 - 27.

28. *An Autobiography,* II, 197.

29. *An Autobiography,* II, 558, 513.

30. *An Autobiography,* II, 557 - 62.

31. *An Autobiography,* II, 197. *Essays,* II, 91.

32. *Essays,* I, 60.

33. Guthrie, *On Mr. Spencer's Unification of Knowledge,* p. 75. Iverach, p. 111.

34. Cargill Gilston Knott, *Life and Scientific Work of Peter Guthrie Tait* (Cambridge, 1911), p. 285. The nebular hypothesis was generally accepted until the 1920's: Joe D. Burchfield, *Lord Kelvin and the Age of the Earth* (New York, 1975), pp. 50, 202.

35. Guthrie, p. 148.

36. Ibid., p. 128. Harris, p. 11. William James, "Great Men, Great Thoughts, and the Environment" (1880), in *The Will to Believe* (New York, 1897), p. 254q. ("pre-Galilean age").

37. James Ward, *Naturalism and Agnosticism* (London, 1903), I, 236 - 37.

38. Iverach, p. 111.

39. *First Principles,* pp. 251, 252, 425, 510; also pp. 454, 477. Guthrie, p. 177 (" 'Abracadabra' ").

40. Beatrice Webb, p. 262.

41. Guthrie, p. 59. Ward, I, p. 261.

42. *First Principles,* pp. 194 - 228. *The Later Letters of John Stuart Mill,* ed. Francis E. Mineka and Dwight N. Lindley, in *Collected Works* (Toronto, 1972), XV, 901. Mill objected to Whewell's emphases on *a priori* ideas and on deduced hypotheses, and in *First Principles* Spencer showed similar emphases.

43. Knott, p. 254.

44. Duncan, p. 430. Guthrie, p. 112.

45. Guthrie, *On Mr. Spencer's Formula of Evolution,* pp. 136 - 37. James, pp. 133 - 34.

46. "Appendix," *First Principles,* p. 554.

47. Knott, p. 286.

48. Guthrie, *On Mr. Spencer's Unification of Knowledge,* p. 89.

49. Ibid., p. 123. Cf. *First Principles,* p. 498.

50. Josiah Royce, *Herbert Spencer* (New York, 1904), p. 112. Thomas Munro, *Evolution in the Arts* (Cleveland, 1963), pp. 64 - 65. George

Gaylord Simpson, *The Meaning of Evolution* (1949) (New Haven, 1967), p. 253.

51. Lester Frank Ward, "Cosmic and Organic Evolution," *Popular Science Monthly,* 11 (1877), 677, 681. Joseph Needham, *Integrative Levels: A Revaluation of the Idea of Progress* (1937), in *Time: The Refreshing River* (London, 1943), p. 247n. Spencer's explanation of "nerve current" also missed the point that the conversion of chemical energy into heat is irreversible: *The Principles of Psychology,* I, 520 - 20*a*. P. B. Medawar, "Onwards from Spencer," *Encounter,* 21 (1963), 37.

52. James, p. 132. Cf. "radical physicalism": Herbert Feigl, "Unity of Science and Unitary Science," in *Readings in the Philosophy of Science,* ed. H. F. and Mary Brodbeck (New York, 1953), pp. 382 - 84.

53. Duncan, p. 104.

54. James Ward, I, 321.

55. Ward, pp. 196 - 97. Merz, II, 288n., 365 - 66, IV, 705, 707. Cf. *First Principles,* pp. 522 - 27. Spencer's lack of university training in mathematics would have prevented him from following the physical sciences in the second half of the century: see Harold I. Sharlin, *The Convergent Century: The Unification of Science in the Nineteenth Century* (New York, 1966), p. 27.

56. Cf. Sixth Edition (New York, 1902), p. 256, and on p. 493, "no actual philosophy can fill out the scheme of an ideal philosophy."

57. Bertrand Russell, "Scientific Method in Philosophy" (Oxford, 1914), pp. 10 - 11. James Ward, I, 189.

58. Munro cited seven writers: pp. 165, 170, 173, 217 - 19.

59. George Eliot, *The Mill on the Floss* (1860) (Boston, 1961), p. 239q. Cf. T. H. Huxley, "On a Piece of Chalk" (1868), *Collected Essays,* VIII, 1 - 36.

60. *First Principles* impressed in this way strong-minded writers like Arnold Bennett, Theodore Dreiser, Hamlin Garland, and Olive Schreiner. See Chapter Nine.

61. Cf. B. F. Skinner, *Beyond Freedom and Dignity* (New York, 1971), pp. 143 - 44, 150 - 51, 211. On Spencer and functionalism: Robert M. Young, "Darwinism and the Division of Labour," *The Listener,* 2264 (17 Aug 1972), 204; "The Role of Psychology in the Nineteenth Century Evolutionary Debate," p. 197; J. D. Y. Peel, *Herbert Spencer* (New York, 1971), p. 210.

Chapter Four

1. *An Autobiography* (New York, 1904), I, 536.

2. *The Principles of Psychology* (New York, 1899), Cited in this chapter as "P." The second edition was an expansion of the first. The only confusing change was that Parts I and II of the first edition were enlarged into Parts VII and VI in Vol. II of the second. The third edition, cited here, was little different from the second.

3. In the 1840's, Spencer had written essays on phrenology. By 1852 only the last pages of "The Philosophy of Style" reflected faculty psychology; the rest was associational psychology. George Bion Denton, "Early Psychological Theories of Herbert Spencer," *American Journal of Psychology,* 32 (1921), 5 - 15. Robert M. Young, *Mind, Brain and Adaptation in the Nineteenth Century* (Oxford, 1970), p. 166.

4. Young, pp. 178 - 79.

5. British Museum MS 36888, pp. 542 - 47, 550 - 60. *An Autobiography,* I, 543. Robert M. Young, "The Development of Herbert Spencer's Concept of Evolution," *Eleventh International Congress on the History of Science* (Warsaw, 1965), I, 79q.

6. David Duncan, *The Life and Letters of Herbert Spencer* (London, 1908), p. 75.

7. Q. by Francis Darwin, *Life and Letters of Charles Darwin* (New York, 1897), I, 542.

8. Morse Peckham, ed., *'The Origin of Species' by Charles Darwin: A Variorum Text* (Philadelphia, 1959), p. 757.

9. "The Belfast Address" (1874), *Fragments of Science* (New York, 1899), II, 173n. *An Autobiography,* I, 546 (Lewes). Duncan, p. 81 (Mill).

10. *The Later Letters of John Stuart Mill, 1849 - 73,* ed. Francis E. Mineka and Dwight N. Lindley, in *Collected Works* (Toronto, 1972), XV, 935. Mill also wrote other praise for Spencer to their friends Alexander Bain and George Grote: *ibid.,* 936; XVI, 1210.

11. Duncan, pp. 140q.,143; Dr. Henry Maudsley was the writer.

12. Duncan, p. 67.

13. "Views Concerning Copyright" (1877), in *Facts and Comments,* pp. 24 - 25.

14. *An Autobiography,* I, 543.

15. Ralph Barton Perry, *The Thought and Character of William James* (1948) (New York, 1964), p. 144.

16. Young, *Mind, Brain and Adaptation,* pp. 197 - 203; "Scholarship and the History of the Behavioural Sciences," *History of Science,* 5 (1966), 21, 5 (1966), 21, 29. Duncan, p. 274. Sir Geoffrey Jefferson, *Selected Papers* (Springfield, Ill. 1960), p. 36. H. W. Magoun, Evolutionary Concepts of Brain Function Following Darwin and Spencer," in *Evolution After Darwin,* ed. Sol Tax (Chicago, 1960), II, 207q., 193.

17. "Preface," *The Factors of Organic Evolution* (New York, 1895), p. v.

18. Darwin referred to the four chapters on the genesis of the nervous system (P, I, 511 - 57): (Chicago, 1965), p. 29n., 71, 198.

19. *An Autobiography,* II, 490q.

20. 'James, *Principles of Psychology* (1890) (New York, 1892), I, 149n. Cf. John Fiske, *Outlines of Cosmic Philosophy* (New York, 1874), II, 444.

21. Duncan, p. 179.

22. Cf. *Essays* (New York, 1899), I, 61. P, I, 147q.

23. In the first edition, Spencer had not been sure that relations were feelings: P, II, 264; II, 285 has "transition state *x*."

24. *Essays*, 241 - 64.
25. Duncan, p. 179q.
26. William James, "Great Men, Great Thoughts, and Environment," (1880), in *The Will to Believe* (New York, 1897), pp. 245, 253.
27. Herbert Dingle, "The Scientific Outlook in 1851 and in 1951," *British Journal for the Philosophy of Science*, 2 (1951), 94.
28. B. D. Burns, *The Uncertain Nervous System* (London, 1968), Chapter 1.
29. J. B. S. Haldane, "Natural Selection," in *Darwin's Biological Work*, ed. P. R. Bell (1959) (New York, 1964), pp. 143 - 44. George John Romanes, *Mental Evolution in Animals* (New York, 1898), pp. 256 - 62.
30. William James entered the social objection to Spencer's view of mind as "pure product" in "Remarks on Spencer's Definition of Mind as Correspondence" (1878), in *Collected Essays and Reviews* (London, 1920), pp. 51q., 53, 67.
31. I. P. Pavlov, "An Attempt to Understand the Symptoms of Hysteria Physiologically," in *Conditioned Reflexes and Psychiatry*, tr. W. H. Gantt (New Yor, 1941), pp. 113 - 14.
32. Eric C. Lenneberg, *Biological Foundations of Language* (New York, 1967).
33. "The Philosophy of Style," *Essays*, II, 335q. *The Principles of Psychology*, II, 124 - 25, a revision of "The Genesis of Science," *Essays*, II, 31 - 33.
34. P, I, 183; II, 513, 409n.q. *First Principles*, p. 196n.q.
35. Benjamin Lee Whorf, *Language, Thought, and Reality* (1956) (Cambridge, Mass., 1964), pp. 57 - 64, 137 - 59, 207 - 19, 233 - 70.
36. "The Genesis of Science" (1854), *Essays*, II, 62. He quoted William Whewell, who had emphasized that scientists made discoveries by inventing conceptions and hypotheses: A. W. Heathcote, "William Whewell's Philosophy of Science," *British Journal of the Philosophy of Science*, 4 (1953 - 54), 302 - 14. Spencer also quoted Whewell in *First Principles*, pp. 373 - 74.
37. Alan Hart, "The Synthetic Epistemology of Herbert Spencer," Doctoral dissertation, University of Pennsylvania, 1965, p. 84. Spencer's essay took a position between the empiricism of Mill and William Whewell's advocacy of "Fundamental Ideas," innate ideas from which the necessary truths of science were intuited. E. W. Strong, "William Whewell and John Stuart Mill: Their Controversy about Scientific Knowledge," *Journal of the History of Ideas*, 16 (1955), 209 - 31. P. B. Medawar, "Hypothesis and Imagination," in *The Art of the Soluble* (London, 1967), pp. 135 - 37, 141 - 42, 145.
38. Henry Sidgwick, "Incoherence of Empirical Philosophy," *Mind*, 7 (1882), 540.
39. "The Universal Postulate," *Westminster Review*, American Edition, 58 (July-October 1853), 271 - 73. Spencer thought he had support in tests of conception advocated by Sir William Hamilton ("unity of representa-

tion") and Henry L. Mansel ("presentable in an intuition"), *ibid.*, p. 286. *The Principles of Psychology*, II, 360. William Whewell had proposed a similar test for hypotheses—the impossibility of distinctly conceiving their negation—in his *Philosophy of the Inductive Sciences* (1840).

40. "The Universal Postulate," pp. 287, 275.

41. "Universal Postulate," pp. 283, 274.

42. J. W. Burrow, *Evolution and Society* (Cambridge, 1966), p. 211. J. D. Y. Peel, *Herbert Spencer* (New York, 1971), pp. 122, 117. Robert Edward Moore, "Spencer's Naturalistic Theory of Ethics," Doctoral dissertation, University of Pennsylvania, 1969, p. 15. Chauncey Wright, "The Philosophy of Herbert Spencer" (1865), in *Philosophical Discussions*, ed. Charles E. Eliot (New York, 1878), p. 67. George Santayana, "The Unknowable" (Oxford, 1923), p. 27.

43. "The Universal Postulate," p. 276. Duncan, p. 121.

44. *A System of Logic*, Eighth Edition (New York, 1895), p. 199.

45. *The Later Letters*, XVI, pp. 1110 - 11, Mill's italics.

46. Mill may not have seen this clearly. The form that he gave can be negated: "trying not to see and not seeing" also yields a conception of darkness. At least, he did not make the point to Spencer. See Leslie Stephen's comment on the controversy: *The English Utilitarians, III: John Stuart Mill* (1900) (New York, 1968), pp. 107 - 08. Also, Alan Ryan, *J. S. Mill* (London, 1974), pp. 63, 71, 220.

47. "Mill *versus* Hamilton—The Test of Truth" (1865), *Essays*, II, 211 - 12q. Italics in this paragraph have been added by the present writer.

48. Alvar Ellegard, *Darwin and the General Reader* (Göteborg, 1958), pp. 179, 181.

49. Letter to Harald Höffding, 18 December 1876, Duncan, pp. 178 - 80q.

50. Duncan, pp. 178, 180. *First Principles*, pp. 500 - 01, 223, 550, 194. In the Sixth Edition of *First Principles*, he omitted talk of transformation, but still allowed an "indirect" quantitative correlation between motion and feeling (New York, 1902), pp. 201q., 197.

51. Tait's "Lecture on Force" showed that force could be measured either as the space rate at which potential energy changed into kinetic energy or as the time rate of change in the momentum of mass in a gravitational field. Cargill Gilston Knott, *Life and Scientific Work of Peter Guthrie Tait* (Cambridge, 1911), p. 288.

52. *First Principles*, p. 193n. Spencer insisted that "force" must refer to an agent, not a rate, of change: *ibid.*, pp. 553 - 54. In 1864, he had noted that in the "Abstract Sciences"—mathematics and logic—"force" was "not only not vital, but [was] studiously not recognized." Spencer, to his loss, did not pursue these sciences. "The Classification of the Sciences," *Essays*, II, 99q., 85.

53. Knott, p. 192, quoting *First Principles*, Second Edition (1867).

54. *First Principles*, pp. 199q., 198.

55. *First Principles*, p. 200.

56. *First Principles,* p. 196n. *The Principles of Psychology,* II, p. 237. Hector Macpherson put it that Spencer started with the intuitions of subjective and objective existence: Duncan, p. 516. But Spencer thought that he could derive belief in subject and object from Cause and from feelings of muscular tension, which symbolized Cause. "Cause in our conception has for its ultimate symbol the relation in consciousness between the sense of effort and any change which we produce by effort; and we use that subjective relation as a symbol for all objective relations of Cause" (1899), Duncan, p. 402. Cf. *First Principles,* pp. 174 - 76. Roger Smith has indicated that A. R. Wallace saw force in objective existence and that Alexander Bain correlated force with muscular tension: "Alfred Russel Wallace: Philosopher of Nature and Man," *British Journal for the History of Science,* 6 (1973), 187 - 88.

57. Burrow, p. 212.

58. Hart, pp. 16, 121. Henry Sidgwick, "Philosophy and Physical Science," *The Academy,* 4 (1873), 133 - 34.

59. "Replies to Criticisms," (1873), *Essays,* II, 241 - 42.

60. Hart, pp. 182, 197, 200.

61. James Ward, *Naturalism and Agnosticism* (London, 1903), I, 270 - 71q. For Ward, the boomerang demolished Spencer's "first starting point" in *First Principles,* where he had presented processes of matter and motion as modes of the Unknowable.

62. Alexander Bain, "Mr. Spencer's Psychological Congruities, II," *Mind,* 6 (1881), 401 - 05.

63. "The Universal Postulate," p. 287.

64. "Replies to Criticisms" (1873), *Essays,* II, 270q., 273, 274n., 298.

65. *Essays,* II, 288.

66. Burrow, p. 211.

67. Hart, p. 155. *An Autobiography,* I, 17.

68. Hart, p. 144.

69. *First Principles,* pp. 499 - 500.

70. The last stage of this logical circle appeared in *The Principles of Sociology,* III, 171: "The last stage reached [by thought] is recognition of the truth that force as it exists beyond consciousness, cannot be like what we know as force within consciousness; and that yet, as either is capable of generating the other, they must be different modes of the same."

71. J. B. Stallo, "Primary Concepts of Modern Physical Science," *Popular Science Monthly,* 4 (1874), 108.

72. *First Principles,* 146q.

73. In this way, as in his postulate of an Absolute Cause, Spencer, the evolutionist, came close to the position of William Whewell, opponent of evolution, who held that hypotheses must be " 'close to the facts,' " and that there must be a Supreme Cause (God). Ellegard, pp. 184 - 85.

74. "Replies to Criticisms," *Essays,* II, 277.

75. *Essays,* II, *315 - 16, 278q.*

76. Knott, pp. 279 - 82.
77. *Essays*, II, 316.
78. *First Principles*, p. 196n. q.
79. Stallo, p. 47.
80. *The Origin of Species*, First Edition, ed. J. W. Burrow (Baltimore, 1968), p. 219.
81. Hart, pp. 50, 127.
82. Robert M. Young, "Scholarship and the History of the Behavioural Sciences," pp. 23 - 24 (Hartley on vibrations in the nerves paralleling association); "The Role of Psychology in the Nineteenth Century Evolutionary Debate," in Mary Henle, et al., eds., *Historical Conceptions of Psychology* (New York, 1973), p. 198 (Berkeley on touch).
83. John Fiske, *Edward Livingston Youmans* (New York, 1894), p. 127.
84. The speeches are available in George Basalla, William Coleman, and Robert A. Kargon, eds., *Victorian Science* (New York, 1970).
85. "The Filiation of Ideas" (1899), in Duncan, p. 548.

Chapter Five

1. *The Principles of Ethics* (New York, 1898), I, xiv. Cited in this chapter as 'E.'
2. *An Autobiography* (New York, 1904), II, 369.
3. John Fiske, *Edward Livingston Youmans* (New York, 1894), pp. 353 - 54.
4. *Evolution and Ethics and Other Essays, Collected Essays* (1894) (Hildesheim, 1970), IX, 79.
5. *First Principles*, Fourth Edition (New York, 1958), pp. 511 - 29. *The Principles of Sociology* (New York, 1898), I, 96.
6. *Social Statics* (1851) (New York, 1954), p. 35. Cited in this chapter as 'S.'
7. *An Autobiography*, II, 100 - 02, 101q. In *The Study of Sociology* (1873) (Ann Arbor, Mich., 1961), he said that "a utilitarian system of ethics" was "visionary," since it could not "be rightly thought out even by the select few": p. 279.
8. The actual difference was that the early Utilitarians, who also aimed to deduce laws for conduct, held that human nature was uniform and simple: Elie Halévy, *The Growth of Philosophic Radicalism*, tr. Mary Morris (Boston, 1955), pp. 494 - 99; J. W. Burrow, *Evolution and Society* (Cambridge, 1966), pp. 215 - 18. The later Mill replied that although he also favored "general principles," he could not agree that they would be "necessary" or that conclusions drawn from them could be "even (absolutely) universal": *The Later Letters of John Stuart Mill, 1849 - 73*, ed. Francis E. Mineka and Dwight N. Lindley, *Collected Works* (Toronto, 1972), XV, 846.
9. *An Autobiography*, II, 101q. *The Principles of Psychology* (New York, 1899), II, 620. Cited in this chapter as "P."

10. Spencer had read Smith's *Theory of Moral Sentiments* in 1843: *An Autobiography*, I, 263.

11. Robert Edward Moore, "Spencer's Naturalistic Theory of Ethics," Doctoral dissertation, University of Pennsylvania, 1969, p. 83.

12. *Social Statics*. Revised Edition (New York, 1892), pp. 23 - 24n.

13. Kate Gordon, "Spencer's Theory of Ethics in its Evolutionary Aspect," *The Philosophical Review*, 11 (1902), 592 - 606.

14. Spencer located the discontents of civilization in the conflict of indoor, sedentary, industrial activities with the anti-social, "remotely inherited and deeply organized feelings" for "a varied life in the open air": *The Principles of Psychology*, I, 282.

15. Robert Edward Moore, p. 117q.

16. *An Autobiography*, I, 570. John Tyndall thought that Spencer would "be a much nicer fellow if he had a good swear now and then": David Duncan, *The Life and Letters of Herbert Spencer* (London, 1908), p. 510.

17. Spencer intended that "survival of the fittest" should have a moral meaning of better or worse in *The Principles of Ethics*. So he had recommended that the moral education of children should emphasize their experiencing "the true consequences of their conduct": *Education* (1861) (London, 1911), pp. 93q., 110.

18. Sidgwick thought that Spencer dated sympathy too late: *Lectures on Ethics* (London, 1902), p. 267. Emile Durkheim objected that altruism existed "from the beginning of humanity and even in a truly intemperate form": *The Division of Labor in Society* (1893), tr. George Simpson (1933) (New York, 1964), pp. 197q., 198, 228, 279.

19. Robert L. Trivers, "The Evolution of Reciprocal Altruism," *The Quarterly Review of Biology*, 46 (1971), pp. 49, 48.

20. He spoke only of "moral" pain and anger, not of reasons for the emotional state: *The Principles of Psychology*, II, 548, 551.

21. Duncan, p. 199. Wilma George, *Biologist Philosopher* (London, 1964), p. 89.

22. *The Malay Archipelago* (1869), Revised Edition (1890) (New York, 1962), pp. 456 - 57. Spencer noticed "certain absolutely peaceful peoples": *The Principles of Ethics*, I, 399q., 471 - 72.

23. In *Principia Ethica*, G. E. Moore skinned Spencer for his omissions, but he did not consider why Spencer left out ethical arguments (Cambridge, 1903), pp. 48 - 58. A. G. N. Flew does not explore why there is a "deficiency of substance" in Spencer's ethics: *Evolutionary Ethics* (London, 1967), p. 43. William James, "Spencer's *Data of Ethics*" (1879), *Collected Essays and Reviews* (London, 1920), p. 149. Francis Gribble, "Herbert Spencer," *Fortnightly Review*, 75 (1904), 993 - 94.

24. Henry Sidgwick, "Mr. Spencer's Ethical System," *Mind*, 5 (1880), 219. Robert Edward Moore, p. 209.

25. *The Principles of Ethics* (London 1893), II, v.

26. "The Theory of Evolution in its Application to Practice," *Mind*, 1 (1876), 57.

27. Alistair MacIntyre, "Hume on 'Is' and 'Ought,'" *Philosophical Review*, 68 (1959), 462 - 68.

28. Duncan, pp. 330 - 37, 334q.

29. *Evolution of Ethics and Other Essays*, pp. 62, 87 - 88, 91 - 92, 82.

30. Oma Stanley, "T. H. Huxley's Treatment of Nature," *Journal of the History of Ideas*, 18 (1957), 120 - 27. "Nature," ed. J. M. Robson, *Collected Works of John Stuart Mill* (Toronto, 1969), X, 396 - 98.

31. *An Autobiography*, II, 168. Huxley's political motives have been clarified by Michael S. Helfand, "T. H. Huxley's 'Evolution and Ethics': The Politics of Evolution and the Evolution of Politics," *Victorian Studies*, 20 (1977), 159 - 77.

32. "The Factors of Organic Evolution," *Essays*, I, 464.

33. Cf. Geoffrey Best, *Mid-Victorian Britain, 1851 - 1875* (London, 1971), pp. 136 - 37.

34. On Potter, Walter E. Houghton, *The Victorian Frame of Mind, 1830 - 1870* (New Haven, 1957), p. 193. On respectability, Houghton, pp. 187 - 88; Best, pp. 260 - 61.

35. William Makepeace Thackeray, *Vanity Fair* (1848) (Boston, 1973), pp. 170q., 124 (chs. 18, 14). Cf. Houghton, p. 192.

Chapter Six

1. *The Principles of Biology* (New York, 1900), II, part V. Darwin's praise was ambiguous, however: Spencer was "a dozen times my superior, even in the master art of wriggling": Francis Darwin, *Life and Letters of Charles Darwin* (New York, 1897), II, 239.

2. *The Later Letters of John Stuart Mill*, ed. Francis E. Mineka and Dwight N. Lindley, in *Collected Works* (Toronto, 1972), XVI, 1505.

3. *The Principles of Biology* (New York, 1898), I, 498. Volume and page numbers in this chapter are to this edition.

4. David Hull, "The Metaphysics of Evolution," *British Journal for the History of Science*, 3 (1967), 335 - 37q.; "What Philosophy of Biology Is Not," *Journal of the History of Biology*, 2 (1969), 255.

5. *The Origin of Species* (1859), ed. J. W. Burrow (Baltimore, 1968), pp. 236, 262.

6. *Origin*, p. 173q. Hull, p. 333. Alvar Ellegard, *Darwin and the General Reader* (Göteborg, 1958), pp. 254 - 55, 274, 334 - 35.

7. Darwin, *Life and Letters*, II, 301 (the young biologist was E. Ray Lankester); "years of work" q. by Raphael Meldola, "Evolution: Darwinian and Spencerian" (Oxford, 1910), p. 29.

8. *An Autobiography* (New York, 1904), I, 201. Charles Coulston Gillispie, *Genesis and Geology* (Cambridge, Mass., 1951), p. 174; "Lamarck and Darwin in the History of Science," in *Forerunners of Darwin, 1745 - 1859*, ed. Bentley Glass et al. (1959) (Baltimore, 1968), pp. 270 - 71. At first, A. R. Wallace also argued for Lamarck and against Lyell: H. Lewis McKinney, *Wallace and Natural Selection* (New Haven, 1972), p. 148.

9. "Letter IV," p. 13, also p. 35. Sir Charles Lyell, *Principles of Geology* (1830 - 33), Eleventh Edition (New York, 1877), II, chapter 36, 296 - 97; Lyell's treatment of Lamarck appeared in chapters 34 - 35. Conway Zirkle, "The Early History of the Idea of the Inheritance of Acquired Characters and of Pangenesis," *Transactions of the American Philosophical Society*, 35 (1946), 91 - 151.

10. "Theory of Life," in *The Complete Works of Samuel Taylor Coleridge*, ed. W. G. T. Shedd (New York, 1885), I, 391 - 92. *Social Statics* (1851) (New York, 1958), pp. 391 -94, 403 - 06.

11. *An Autobiography,* I, 436. David Duncan, *The Life and Letters of Herbert Spencer* (London, 1908), p. 542. Henri Milne-Edwards advanced his view in 1827: John Theodore Merz, *A History of European Thought in the Nineteenth Century* (1903), Third Edition (Edinburgh, 1928), II, 322n.

12. "The Development Hypothesis," *Essays* (New York, 1899), I, 29.

13. Duncan, p. 87.

14. *An Autobiography,* I, 445, 450.

15. *Westminster Review,* American Edition, 57 (April 1852), 255, 252, 261, 262 - 63; partially reprinted in *The Principles of Biology,* I, 577 - 601. Aristotle and Carpenter had observed an opposition between size or nutrition and reproduction, but Spencer was unaware of their ideas in 1852: ibid., II, 460n.; Zirkle, p. 126. Spencer's correlation of phosphorus in neural and sperm cells had its analogues in Hippocrates' and St. Albert Magnus's correlations of the brain and coition: Zirkle, p. 127; *The Principles of Biology,* I, 596 - 97.

16. *Westminster Review,* pp. 267, 266. D. E. C. Eversley reported that Spencer's view of an equilibrium in human population had wide influence in the United States, France, and England: *Social Theories of Fertility and the Malthusian Debate* (Oxford, 1959), p. 190.

17. *An Autobiography,* I, 451 - 52.

18. Peter Vorzimmer, "Darwin, Malthus and the Theory of Natural Selection," *Journal of the History of Ideas,* 30 (1969), 527 - 42, especially p. 538. Spencer's letter to Darwin, 22 February 1860, q. in *Sir Charles Lyell's Scientific Journals on the Species Question,* ed. Leonard G. Wilson (New Haven, 1970), pp. 353 - 54.

19. *Essays,* I, 48, 85.

20. *Essays,* I, 51, 91q. Spencer's italics.

21. *The Principles of Biology,* II, 565: "A Criticism on Professor Owen's Theory of the Vertebrate Skeleton."

22. *An Autobiography,* II, 119.

23. "On Circulation and the Formation of Wood in Plants," *The Principles of Biology,* II, 567 - 90. A. R. Wallace, q. by Meldola, p. [44] q.

24. *An Autobiography,* II, 150.

25. *Autobiography,* II, 165 - 66.

26. *The Principles of Biology,* I, 15 - 16, 41, 63. The great change in

modern biochemistry has been the recognition of "complementarity" as the principle of "structure" in the molecules of living things: P. B. Medawar, *The Art of the Soluble* (London, 1967), pp. 41, 105.

27. Duncan, p. 144. More recent accounts are Lawrence J. Henderson, "Life and the Cosmos," in *The Fitness of the Environment* (1927) (Boston, 1958), and A. I. Oparin, *Life: Its Nature, Origins, and Development*, tr. A. Synge (New York, 1964), chapters 2, 3.

28. James D. Watson, *Molecular Biology of the Gene*, Second Edition (New York, 1970), pp. 48q., 49, 58 - 59.

29. Watson, p. 67.

30. *First Principles*, Fourth Edition (New York, 1954), pp. 479 - 84.

31. T. A. Goudge, *The Ascent of Life: A Philosophical Study of the Theory of Evolution* (Toronto, 1961), pp. 107 - 08q. George Gaylord Simpson, *The Meaning of Evolution* (1949) (New Haven, 1967), p. 268.

32. Also in *The Principles of Psychology* (New York, 1899), II, 7 - 8, 96; "The Nebular Hypothesis," *Essays*, I, 145. August Weismann and J. Arthur Thomson said that Rudolf Leuckart first noted this limit of growth: *Essays on Heredity*, ed. E. B. Poulton, tr. S. Schönland and A. E. Shipley (Oxford, 1891), I, 7; *Herbert Spencer* (London, 1906), p. 112. Robert L. Carneiro noted that Galileo had observed the facts: *The Evolution of Society* (Chicago, 1967), p. xiv; Galileo, *Dialogues Concerning Two New Sciences*, tr. Henry Crew and Alfonso De Salvio (1914) (New York, 1952), pp. 130 - 33.

33. P. B. Medawar has pointed out that organisms circumvent the disproportion by folded surfaces and high metabolism: *The Uniqueness of the Individual* (New York: 1957), p. 113.

34. Merz credited Spencer with the first "mechanical explanation of the process of cellular division": II, p. 445.

35. Thomson, p. 116.

36. Cf. *Essays*, I, p. 77 (1857). Joseph Needham, *Integrative Levels: A Revaluation of the Idea of Progress* (Oxford, 1937), p. 23.

37. Goudge, pp. 85 - 86.

38. Goudge, pp. 94, 111 - 12.

39. Duncan, p. 151. Some awareness of the double helix structure of the DNA molecule, of the mechanisms of immunity, and of species-characteristic configurations of amino acids makes Spencer's hypothesis seem prescient. Cf. Medawar, *The Art of the Soluble*, pp. 162 - 65.

40. A difficulty was that even in lower animals regeneration did not always take place or was restricted to one part or one cell type. Natural selection has determined whether an animal has genetic determinants for regeneration: Thomson, p. 161; Weismann, *The Germ Plasm: A Theory of Heredity* (1892), tr. W. N. Parker and H. Rönnfeldt (New York, 1898), p. 128.

41. He did not live to see Einstein explain gravitation by inertia, not by

"force" acting through immense distances through an imponderable ether: Lincoln Barnett, *The Universe and Dr. Einstein* (New York, 1948), pp. 34 - 36 and chapter 11.

42. Needham praised this acknowledgement of "autogenous development," *Integrative Levels*, p. 24.

43. Spencer had first noticed that inheritance was not just a blending, but an "irregular combination of characteristics" from the parents, in "Personal Beauty" (1854), *Essays*, II, 395.

44. Peter Vorzimmer, "Charles Darwin and Blending Inheritance," *Isis*, 55 (1963), 386. Weismann, *The Germ Plasm*, pp. 6, 104.

45. William Coleman, "Cell, Nucleus and Inheritance, an Historical Study," *Proceedings of the American Philosophical Society*, 109 (1965), 124 - 58.

46. Thomson, p. 122.

47. In 1866 (Fourth Edition) Darwin referred to Spencer on fertilization in support of his own account of hybrid vigor: Morse Peckham, ed., '*The Origin of Species' by Charles Darwin: A Variorum Text* (Philadelphia, 1959), p. 453.

48. Malcolm Guthrie, *On Mr. Spencer's Unification of Knowledge*, (London, 1882), p. 446. Thomson, p. 123.

49. *Essays*, I, 9, 83.

50. Cf Elizabeth Gashing, "Why Was Mendel's Work Ignored?" *Journal of the History of Ideas*, 20 (1959), 60 - 83.

51. Thomson, pp. 106, 116.

52. P. B. Medawar, "Herbert Spencer and the Law of General Evolution" (1963), in *The Art of the Soluble*, p. 44q.

53. James Allen Rodgers, "Darwinism and Social Darwinism," *Journal of the History of Ideas*, 33 (1972), 274.

54. Cf. *Essays*, I, 408.

55. Goudge, pp. 115 - 16.

56. *The Origin of Species*, p. 119q. Barry G. Gale, "Darwin and the Concept of a Struggle for Existence: A Study in the Extrascientific Origins of Scientific Ideas," *Isis*, 63 (1972), 321 - 44.

57. *The Origin of Species*, p. 459. Cf. Darwin, *The Descent of Man* (1871) (New York, 1897), pp. 143, 145.

58. Ernest Mayr, "Isolation as an Evolutionary Factor," *Proceedings of the American Philosophical Society*, 103 (1959), 221 - 30. Hull, "The Metaphysics of Evolution," pp. 336 - 37.

59. A. R. Wallace recommended the term to Darwin in 1866, and it appeared in the title and first sentence of Chapter III of the Fifth Edition (1869) of *The Origin of Species:* Wilma George, *Biologist Philosopher* (London, 1964); Peckham, p. 145q.

60. *An Autobiography*, II, 115q.

61. Goudge, pp. 117 - 18.

62. Hull, "What Philosophy of Biology Is Not," pp. 253 - 54.

63. *Essays*, I, 379 (1872), 430 (1886).

64. J. S. Wilkie, "Buffon, Lamarck and Darwin," in *Darwin's Biological Work* (1959), ed. P. R. Bell (New York, 1964), p. 297.

65. *The Origin of Species*, p. 262. Vorzimmer, p. 389. *The Descent of Man*, pp. 33, 131. Darwin turned to use-inheritance to meet the time limits calculated by William Thomson, Lord Kelvin: Joe D. Burchfield, *Lord Kelvin and the Age of the Earth* (New York, 1975), p. 76.

66. E. B. Poulton, *Essays on Evolution, 1889 - 1907* (Oxford, 1908), pp. 143 - 44.

67. Medawar, "A Commentary on Lamarckism," in *The Uniqueness of the Individual*, p. 85. C. H. Waddington, *The Nature of Life* (New York, 1962), pp. 91, 97.

68. *Essays*, I, 391.

69. Thomson, p. 260. Conway Zirkle has shown that no one before Darwin saw the combination of individual variation and natural selection that Darwin saw: "Natural Selection before the 'Origin of Species,' " *Proceedings of the American Philosophical Society*, 84 (1941), 71 - 123.

70. *The Origin of Species*, p. 227.

71. Michael T. Ghiselin, *The Triumph of the Darwinian Method* (Berkeley, 1969), pp. 170, 229, 240, 61.

72. The philosopher Marjorie Grene is a recent example of a thinker who cannot accept correlated growth: "The Faith of Darwinism," *Encounter*, 13 (1959), 54.

73. Ghiselin, "The Individual in the Darwinian Revolution," *New Literary History*, 3 (1971 - 72), 129. Ironically, Darwin used Spencer's biology in enlarging his views of correlation of growth in the Fourth and later editions of *The Origin of Species* and *The Variation of Animals and Plants under Domestication* (1868): Peter Vorzimmer, *Charles Darwin: The Years of Controversy* (Philadelphia, 1970), p. 86.

74. *Essays*, I, 478, 430.

75. The equilibria important in evolutionary theory today are "equilibria of gene pools": Richard C. Lewontin, "The Bases of Conflict in Biological Explanation," *Journal of the History of Biology*, 2 (1969), 41 - 43.

76. Cf. *Essays*, I, p. 88.

77. Peckham, p. 225; Darwin q. *The Principles of Biology*, II, 159 - 60.

78. In 1898, Spencer noticed in a footnote Darwin's view that the plumage and songs of birds developed by sexual selection: ibid., 269n.

79. A. R. Wallace was so impressed by Spencer's account of sap motion that he called him the "most illuminating reasoner of the Nineteenth Century": q. Meldola, p. [44].

80. *First Principles*, pp. 199 - 200.

81. Guthrie, p. 375.

82. Thomson, p. 126.

83. Goudge, p. 210.

84. D. E. C. Eversley (note 16), p. 189.
85. Medawar, *The Uniqueness of the Individual*, p. 185.
86. Goudge, p. 139.
87. Eversley, p. 185.
88. *Essays*, I, e. g., 397 - 405.
89. *Essays*, I, 405.
90. *Essays*, I, 455, 458.
91. George, p. 259, q. a letter by A. R. Wallace. Frederick B. Churchill, "August Weismann and a Break from Tradition," *Journal of the History of Biology*, 1 (1968), 91 - 112.
92. He reprinted them all under the title of the first, "The Inadequacy of Natural Selection," as an appendix to Vol. I of *The Principles of Biology*, Second Edition.
93. "Preface" (New York, 1895), p. v.
94. In his psychology, Spencer had also explained that so many superiorities and inferiorities varied independently in people that "natural selection [could] not by itself rectify any particular unfitness." So "the inheritance of functionally-produced alterations [in humans was] slower than it would otherwise be": *The Principles of Psychology*, I, 283 - 84.
95. Alan Hart, "The Synthetic Epistemology of Herbert Spencer," Doctoral dissertation, University of Pennsylvania, 1965, pp. 74 - 76.
96. On Owen, see Ellegard, pp. 48 - 51, 271q.
97. Medawar points out the fallacy of "independent variables": *The Art of the Soluble*, p. 46 and n.
98. "On Heredity" (1883), in *Essays on Heredity*, I, p. 83.
99. "On Heredity," pp. 82 - 91. A. R. Wallace, *Darwinism* (1889) (London, 1896), pp. 411 - 20. Edward J. Pfeifer, "The Genesis of American neo-Lamarckism," *Isis*, 56 (1965), 156 - 67. Lester Frank Ward (a Lamarckian) and William James thought that Spencer had argued well: "Weismann's Concessions," *Popular Science Monthly*, 45 (1894), 175 - 84; "Herbert Spencer's Autobiography," in *Memories and Studies* (London, 1911), p. 140. Most recently, T. S. Lysenko found evolution "unthinkable without recognition of the inheritance of acquired characteristics": *The Situation in Biological Science* (Moscow, 1949), pp. 15q., 16, 37 - 38. Lysenko attacked Weismann; and the views of I. V. Michurin that he supported were like Spencer's: pangenesis and the primacy of external conditions for organic change.
100. *Essays upon Heredity*, I, p. 87.
101. Donald MacRae, "Introduction," *The Man 'versus' the State* (Baltimore, 1969), p. 31.
102. Poulton. p. 99.
103. W. J. Harvey has shown that George Eliot's character does not represent Spencer: *'Middlemarch': Critical Approaches to the Novel*, ed. Barbara Hardy (Oxford, 1967), pp. 30 - 34. Cf. *Middlemarch* (1871 - 72), chapters 20 - 21. On Schwann and Bernard, see Everett Mendelsohn, "Physical Models and Physiological Concepts: Explanation in Nineteenth-

Century Biology," *The British Journal for the History of Science*, 2 (1965), 201 - 19.

104. Goudge, pp. 162 - 63, 166 - 67.

105. Simpson, pp. 253 - 54.

106. George Kimball Plochmann, "Darwin or Spencer," *Science*, 134 (1959), 1456.

107. J. D. Y. Peel, *Herbert Spencer* (New York, 1971), p. 143, italics added.

108. Robert M. Young, "Evolutionary Biology and Ideology: Then and Now," *Science Studies*, I, (1971), 184.

109. Robert M. Young, "Darwin's Metaphor: Does Nature Select?," *The Monist*, 55 (1971), 442 - 503.

Chapter Seven

1. *Social Statics* (1851) (New York, 1954), p. 60.

2. *First Principles*, Fourth Edition (New York, 1958), pp. 537, 394.

3. *First Principles*, p. 316.

4. J. W. Burrow noted that academic study of anthropology and of sociology received university recognition in England only in 1884 and 1903, respectively: *Evolution and Society* (Cambridge, 1966), pp. 81, 235.

5. *An Autobiography* (New York, 1904), II, 285q., 288, 299. *The Study of Sociology*, Seventh Edition (Ann Arbor, Mich., 1961), p. 350. Cited in this chapter as "SS." Philip Abrams, ed., *The Origins of British Sociology, 1834 - 1914* (Chicago, 1968), p. 73.

6. In 1893, he acknowledged that "in the days of early enthusiasm" (1850), he had "thought that all would go well" were there only reforms in government: *An Autobiography*, II, 544.

7. *The Principles of Sociology* (New York, 1898), II, 233. Cited in this chapter as "PS." J. D. Y. Peel, "Spencer and the Neo-Evolutionists," *Sociology*, 3 (1967), 176.

8. Peel, p. 188. Peel, *Herbert Spencer* (New York, 1971), p. 209. Robert G. Perrin finds that Spencer had (only) a populational theory for social change: "Herbert Spencer's Four Theories of Social Evolution," *American Journal of Sociology*, 81 (1976), p. 1354.

9. Peel, *Herbert Spencer*, pp. 183, 191. Burrow, pp. 221 - 22.

10. *First Principles*, p. 133. Cf. *Social Statics*, pp. 424 - 25.

11. Peel, "Spencer and the Neo-Evolutionists," p. 181.

12. The whole peroration seems disingenuous when one realizes that for Spencer developments in national character, not ideas, produced the opinions which worked social changes: see Chapter 8.

13. Everett Knight, *A Theory of the Classical Novel* (New York, 1970), pp. 30, 77, 95, 117. The aphorism of which Matthew Arnold was fond—"force till right is ready"—is exemplary, meaning as it does, "we will use the force, but your right will be wrong until we are ready for it": *Lectures and Essays in Criticism*, in *Complete Prose Works*, ed. R. H. Super (Ann Arbor, Mich., 1962), III, 265 - 66.

14. John Foster has shown that these classes were potent forces for isolating and advancing working class leaders of the 1840's during the 1850's: *Class Struggle and the Industrial Revolution: Early Industrial Capitalism in Three English Towns* (London, 1974), pp. 188 - 91. A careful review of teachers and schools was begun by such "betters": Richard Johnson, "Educational Policy and Social Control in Early Victorian England," *Past and Present*, 49 (1970), 114 - 19. J. M. Goldstrom, *The Social Content of Education, 1808 - 1870* (Shannon, 1972).

15. "Aggregate" appears twenty-nine times in Chapter III of *The Study of Sociology*. John Ruskin objected to Frederic Harrison's use of the word: "an aggregate of men is a mob, and not Humanity. . . . an aggregate of geese is—perhaps you had better consult Mr. Herbert Spencer and the late Mr. John Stuart Mill for the best modern expression." Letter 66 (1876), *Fors Clavigera*, in *The Complete Works*, ed. E. T. Cook and Alexander Wedderburn (London, 1907), XXVIII, 623.

16. David Duncan, *The Life and Letters of Herbert Spencer* (London, 1908), pp. 112, 258, 376. Louis Bruce Fike, "Despotism, Liberty, and Retrogression, The Political Philosophy of Herbert Spencer," Doctoral dissertation, Brown University, 1969, pp. 49 - 59. John C. Greene, "Biology and Social Theory in the Nineteenth Century: Auguste Comte and Herbert Spencer," *Critical Problems in the History of Science*, ed. Marshall Clagett (Madison, 1959), pp. 419 - 46.

17. Jay Rumney, *Herbert Spencer's Sociology* (1934) (New York, 1966), p. 59. A. R. Wallace argued that brain size would have been an injurious variation. Darwin had held that natural selection could be falsified, should it produce any structure in one species "for the exclusive good of another species," or should it "produce in a being anything injurious to itself": *The Origin of Species* (1959), ed. J. W. Burrow (Baltimore, 1968), p. 229. Hence Wallace's point was that natural selection could be falsified, as the cause of man's mental development: Alfred Russel Wallace, "The Limits of Natural Selection as Applied to Man" (1870), in *Natural Selection and Tropical Nature* (1875) (London, 1895), pp. 186 - 93.

18. *Social Statics*, pp. 403 - 08. *The Principles of Psychology* (New York, 1899), II, 76. "Progress: Its Law and Cause" and "Transcendental Physiology," in *Essays* (New York 1899), I, 23, 58, 102 - 06. "The Social Organism," *ibid.*, 265 - 307. "Specialized Administration," *ibid.*, III, 419 - 23.

19. *Essays*, I, 269 - 72. F. W. Coker, *Organismic Theories of the State: Nineteenth Century Interpretations of the State as Organism or as Person* (New York, 1967).

20. *The Principles of Biology* (New York, 1898, 1900), II, 88 - 95.

21. Daniel Carter Carbaugh, "Biological Analogy in the Theories of Françqis Quesnay and Herbert Spencer," Doctoral dissertation, University of Missouri - Kansas City, 1969, p. 323. Morris Ginsberg, *Studies in Sociology* (London, 1932), p. 73. Peel, *Herbert Spencer*, p. 181. Rumney, p.

52. J. Arthur Thomson, *Herbert Spencer* (London, 1906), p. 256.

22. R. A. Fisher, *The Genetical Theory of Natural Selection* (1930) (New York, 1958), pp. 199ff.

23. *An Autobiography*, II, 543.

24. "The Americans: A Conversation" (1882), *Essays*, III, 480. *The Principles of Sociology*, I, 572 - 74. Spencer was the most unconscious of racists. He did not believe that some races were absolutely inferior: *The Principles of Psychology*, I, 461 - 62. Although some had evolved further by their past interaction with environment, all peoples might progress. Nevertheless, it was his practice to regard most non-white peoples as "lower races of men": *ibid.*, 368, 471; *The Principles of Sociology*, II, 647. Peel, *Herbert Spencer*, pp. 144 - 45.

25. "Transcendental Physiology," *Essays*, I, 106.

26. Rumney, p. 236. Lucien Goldmann, "History and Class Consciousness," in *Aspects of History and Class Consciousness*, ed. Istvan Meszaros (London, 1971), pp. 72 - 74.

27. Peel, *Herbert Spencer*, p. 198.

28. Burrow, *Evolution and Society*, p. 203.

29. *Social Statics*, p. 76. "On Manners and fashion" (1854), *Essays*, III, 24. *The Principles of Sociology*, I, 56, 64, 67, 90 - 91, 131. *The Principles of Psychology*, II, 598 - 99, 623.

30. *Principles*, II, 558 - 60.

31. Peel, *Herbert Spencer*, p. 203q., 198, 200.

32 Burrow, *Evolution and Society*, p. 207.

33. *An Autobiography*, II, 306q., 201, 308, 311.

34. "What Knowledge is of most Worth?" (1859), *Education* (1861) (London, 1911), p. 29.

35. *An Autobiography*, II, 252, 411, 412, 414.

36. *Autobiography*, II, 312 - 13. *Various Fragments* (New York, 1898), p. 27.

37. *Autobiography*, II, 414 - 15, 298.

38. *Autobiography*, II, 351.

39. Cf. Lester Frank Ward, *Glimpses of the Cosmos* (New York, 1917), V, 302q., and Margaret Mead, *Cooperation and Competition among Primitive Peoples*, ed. M. Mead, Revised Edition (Boston, 1961), p. 4q.

40. Rumney, pp. 188, 203 - 04.

41. Benjamin Lee Whorf, *Language, Thought, and Reality* (Cambridge, Mass., 1964), pp. 141, 152 - 53.

42. Rumney, pp. 199 - 201.

43. "Mr. Spencer's Principles of Sociology,' " *Mind*, 2(1877), 155 - 56, 420 - 23. *Essays*, I, 310 - 312n.

44. *Mind*, 2 (1877), 423 - 29. He could also point to having implied the idea of doubles of the dead in "On Manners and Fashion" (1854), *Essays*, III, 6.

45. Mind, 2 (1877), 429.

46. Rumney, pp. 102, 110 - 12, 118. David F. Aberle, "Matrilineal Descent in Cross-Cultural Perspective," *Matrilineal Kinship*, ed. David M. Schneider and Kathleen Gough (Berkeley, 1962), pp. 658 - 59.

47. Duncan, p. 569.

48. *An Autobiography*, II, 388 - 89.

49. *Social Statics*, p. 374. "On Manners and Fashion," *Essays*, III, 5, 8 - 11. "Progress: Its Law and Cause," *ibid.*, I, 19 - 20.

50. *An Autobiography*, II, 355. Duncan, p. 571.

51. Burrow noted that in 1828 Thomas R. Edmonds had anticipated Spencer on the beneficent consequences of war: *Evolution and Society*, p. 78n.

52. *An Autobiography*, II, 438q. Duncan, p. 217.

53. David C. Rapoport, "Military and Civil Societies," *Political Studies*, 12 (1964), 178 - 201.

54. *The Principles of Ethics* (New York, 1898), II, 184, 185.

55. Mead, pp. 480, 511q., 481.

56. Peel, "Spencer and the Neo-Evolutionists," p. 188q. Greene, pp. 439 - 40.

57. Karl R. Popper, *The Open Society and Its Enemies* (1944) (Princeton, 1950), pp. 169 - 70.

58. Fike, p. 312. C. Wright Mills, *The Power Elite* (New York, 1956), p. 215. Rumney, p. 89.

59. "The Genesis of Science" (1854), *Essays*, I, 29 - 30.

60. Marshall D. Sahlins and Elman R. Service, eds., *Evolution and Culture* (Ann Arbor, Mich., 1960), pp. 12 - 14, 93 - 122.

61. Peel, *Herbert Spencer*, p. 165.

62. George W. Stocking, Jr., *Race, Culture, and Evolution* (New York, 1968), pp. 126 - 28, 238 - 69, 273 - 307. Jurgen Herbst, "Social Darwinism and the History of American Geography," *Proceedings of the American Philosophical Society*, 105 (1961), 538 - 44. Robert L. Carneiro, "Herbert Spencer's *The Study of Sociology* and the Rise of Social Science in America." *ibid.*, 118 (1974), 540 - 54. Edwin G. Boring, "The Influence of Evolutionary Theory upon American Psychological Thought," in *Evolutionary Thought in America*, ed. Stow Persons (New Haven, 1950), pp. 280 - 82. Werner Stark, "Herbert Spencer's Three Sociologies," *American Sociological Review*, 26 (1961), 519. For the professional context of Spencer's waning influence in the U. S., see Mary O. Furner, *Advocacy and Objectivity: A Crisis in the Professionalization of American Social Science* (Lexington, Kentucky, 1975).

63. Charles Horton Cooley, "Reflections upon the Sociology of Herbert Spencer" (1920), in *Sociological Theory and Social Research* (1930) (New York, 1969), p. 272. Emile Durkheim, *The Division of Labor in Society* (1893), tr. George Simpson (1933) (New York, 1964), pp. 342 - 43. Henry George, *Progress and Poverty* (1880) (New York, 1930), pp. 504 - 05. A. L. Kroeber, "The Superorganic, *American Anthropologist*, New Series 19

(1917), 163 - 213. Rumney, p. 256.

64. Spencer, "The Relations of Biology, Psychology, and Sociology," *Popular Science Monthly*, 50 (1896), 163 - 71.

65. *An Autobiography*, II, 560 - 61.

66. "The Origin and Function of Music" (1857), *Essays*, II, 425 - 26.

67. He used "culture" in a reasonably inclusive sense twice in his sociology: Robert L. Carneiro, *The Evolution of Society* (Chicago, 1967), p. xxxiiin.; *The Principles of Sociology*, II, 568, III, 7. Usually he used the word to mean "education": *ibid.*, I, 112.

68. *Principles*, II, pp. 434, 441. Joseph H. Greenberg, *Essays in Linguistics* (Chicago, 1957), pp. 60 - 61.

69. *The Principles of Psychology*, I, 471q. "The Philosophy of Style," *Essays*, II, 366. *Social Statics*, p. 246. "Progress: Its Law and Cause, *Essays*, I, 23. *First Principles*, p. 321, where Chinese is called an "incoherent" language.

70. Greenberg, "Some Universals of Grammar," in *Universals of Language*, ed. J. H. Greenberg (Cambridge, Mass., 1966), p. 74; "sentences": J. P. B. Allen and Paul Van Buren, eds., *Chomsky: Selected Readings* (Oxford, 1971), pp. 66 - 67.

71. Joyce O. Hertzler, *A Sociology of Language* (New York, 1965), pp. 100 - 02, 116 - 34. Joshua A. Fishman, "A Systematization of the Whorfian Hypothesis," in *Communication and Culture*. ed. Alfred G. Smith (New York, 1966), pp. 508, 514, 516; John B. Carroll and Joseph B. Casagrande, "The Functions of Language Classifications in Behavior," *ibid.*, pp. 491, 504.

Chapter Eight

1. *Social Statics* (1851) (New York, 1954), pp. 191q., 167. Cited in this chapter as "S."

2. *Social Statics*, Abridged and Revised Edition (New York, 1892), p. 116. Harold Issadore Sharlin, "Herbert Spencer and Scientism," *Annals of Science*, 33 (1976), 458.

3. *The Proper Sphere of Government* (London, 1843), pp. 5, 25. Cited in this chapter as "P."

4. J. D. Y. Peel, *Herbert Spencer* (New York, 1971), p. 102.

5. *The Principles of Sociology* (New York, 1898), II, 553 - 54. Cited in this chapter as "PS."

6. Arthur J. Taylor, "The Originality of Herbert Spencer," *University of Texas Studies in English*, 34 (1956), 102 and n.

7. *Labour Defended Against the Claims of Capital* (1825) (New York, 1963), p. 109.

8. Peel, pp. 79 - 80, 83.

9. Scott Gordon, "The London *Economist* and the High Tide of Laissez-Faire," *Journal of Political Economy*, 63 (1955), 478 - 84.

10. Gordon, p. 470.

11. Cf. Paley, *The Principles of Moral and Political Philosophy* (1785) (Cambridge, Mass., 1830), p. 40; on happiness, p. 16.
12. Gordon, pp. 472, 480; 470; 478.
13. Gordon, pp. 465, 480. Louis Bruce Fike, "Despotism, Liberty, and Retrogression," Doctoral dissertation, Brown University, 1969, p. 318.
14. *The Principles of Ethics* (New York, 1898), II, 379. Cited in this chapter as "E."
15. *Labour Defended. . .* , pp. 51 - 2.
16. *Labour Defended. . .* , p. 55. C. H. Driver, "Thomas Hodgskin and the Individualists," *Social and Political Ideas of the Age of Reaction and Reconstruction*, ed. F. J. Hearnshaw (1931) (New York, 1949), pp. 208 - 11.
17. *Labour Defended. . .* , p. 52.
18. *Labour Defended. . .* , p. 109q. *The Natural and Artificial Rights of Property Contrasted* (London, 1832), p. 148.
19. *The Unknown Mayhew*, ed. Eileen Yeo and E. P. Thompson (New York, 1971).
20. David Duncan, *The Life and Letters of Herbert Spencer* (London, 1908), p. 248.
21. *An Autobiography* (New York, 1904), II, 536 - 37. Duncan, pp. 338 - 42.
22. *Progress and Poverty* (1880) (New York, 1930), pp. 59 - 61. *A Perplexed Philosopher* (1892) (New York, 1946), Chapters 4, 5.
23. Hole, pp. 159, 121. On Hole, see J. F. C. Harrison's article in *Dictionary of Labour Biography*, ed. Joyce M. Bellamy and John Saville (London, 1974), II, 183 - 85.
24. *An Autobiography*, I, pp. 76 - 8. J. H. Tremenheere, "The Children's Employment Commission," *Quarterly Review* (1866), in *Victorian Social Conscience: Working Conditions*, ed. John Saville (Westmead, England, 1973), pp. 371 - 72.
25. Hole, p. 123.
26. E. J. Hobsbawn, "The British Standard of Living, 1790 - 1850," *Economic History Review*, 10 (1957), pp. 46 - 60.
27. Hole, p. 145.
28. *The Man 'versus' the State* (1889) (Baltimore, 1969), pp. 315 - 16.
29. Hole, p. 120.
30. Gordon, p. 472. "Inferiors": *Social Statics*, pp. 289, 338; *the Study of Sociology* (Ann Arbor, Mich., 1961), pp. 314 - 15. "Good-for-nothings": *The Man 'versus' the State*, pp. 82, 111. "Jail": Robert Roberts, *The Classic Slum* (Manchester, 1971), pp. 42, 52. "Vagrants": Gareth Stedman Jones, *Outcast London* (Oxford, 1971), p. 89.
31. Hole, pp. 39, 64.
32. Hole, pp. 138 - 39.
33. Hole, pp. 43, 133.
34. *The Man 'versus' the State*, pp. 132, 135.
35. "The Factories," *Westminster Review* (1836), in *Victorian Social Conscience: Working Conditions*, pp. 185 - 86.

36. Fike, pp. 113 - 14.
37. *Social Statics*, pp. 160, 206, 252, 314. Cf "Unpublished Letters," *Independent*, 56 (1904), p. 1004. *The Study of Sociology*, pp. 332 - 33.
38. *The Man 'versus' the State*, pp. 332 - 33.
39. "Replies to Criticisms on *The Data of Ethics*," *Mind*, 6 (1888), 93. Henry Sidgwick, "The Theory of Evolution in its Application to Practice," *Mind*, 1 (1876), 62. Francis Adams, *Essays in Modernity* (London, 1899), p. 70.
40. Duncan, pp. 138 - 39; *The Study of Sociology*, pp. 341 - 47; *The Principles of Sociology*, I, 768 - 69; *The Principles of Ethics*, II, 191 - 97.
41. *An Autobiography*, II, 432, 436q. Duncan, p. 94.
42. Duncan, p. 336.
43. Duncan, p. 335. Spencer has slight influence on the work of contemporary British economists: William L. Miller, "Herbert Spencer's Theory of Welfare and Public Policy," *History of Political Economy*, 4 (1972), 227.
44. Cf. *The Proper Sphere of Government*, p. 35: without "imperious necessity" men "would sink into a state of hopeless torpidity."
45. E. P. Thompson, "Time, Work-discipline and Industrial Capitalism," *Past and Present*, 38 (1967), 56 - 97.
46. Peel, p. 58. Elie Halévy, *The Growth of Philosophic Radicalism*, tr. Mary Morris (1928) (Boston, 1955), p. 190.
47. Jay Rumney, *Herbert Spencer's Sociology* (1934) (New York, 1966), p. 132.
48. Spencer was reading Bentham in 1843: *An Autobiography*, I, 260.
49. Spencer explicitly rejected the social contract theory of the origin of government: *Social Statics*, pp. 180, 226 - 27.
50. *First Principles*, Fourth Edition (New York, 1958), p. 506.
51. Duncan, p. 466.
52. *An Autobiography*, I, 344.
53. Fike, p. 291.
54. *Merrie England* (1894) (New York, 1966), p. 210.
55. *The Study of Sociology*, pp. 217, 367q.
56. *Study*, p. 176.
57. Ernest Barker, *Political Thought in England from Spencer to the Present* (New York, 1915), p. 108q. Also, Rumney, pp. 135 - 37.
58. Duncan, p. 354.
59. *Essays*, (New York, 1899), III, 107. *The Man 'versus' the State*, pp. 245 - 48.
60. *The Man 'versus' the State*, p. 267. *An Autobiography*, I, 513.
61. *Essays*, III, 63 - 64. *Little Dorrit* (1857), Book I, chapter 21; Book II, Chapters 12, 16, 25. F. M. L. Thompson, *English Landed Society in the Nineteenth Century* (London, 1963), pp. 306 - 08.
62. *An Autobiography*, II, 436; cf. *The Proper Sphere of Government*, pp. 21, 32.
63. Duncan, pp. 284, 410. Cf. *The Principles of Ethics*, II, p. 429. Spencer tried to enlist the poet Swinburne in his League's work: William Baker,

"A. C. Swinburne to Herbert Spencer, 12 March 1881: An Unpublished Letter," *Notes and Queries*, n. s., 22 (1975), 445 - 47.

64. *The Principles of Ethics*, II, p. 441. Rumney, p. 89.

65. Duncan, p. 276. Cf. Donald MacRae, "Introduction," *The Man 'versus' the State*, p. 43.

66. Duncan, p. 284.

67. Peel, p. 223q. Hole, p. 39.

68. MacRae, p. 32.

69. MacRae, p. 37. Fike, pp. 326 - 29.

70. *Essays*, II, 138, 143, 148.

71. R. G. Collingwood, *Essays on the Philosophy of History*, ed. William Debbins (Austin, Texas, 1965), pp. 119 - 20.

72. Hole, p. 132.

73. *the Proper Sphere of Government*, p. 36. *The Principles of Sociology*, II, 660. *The Man 'versus' the State*, pp. 306, 307. *Social Statics*, pp. 228 - 29. *The Study of Sociology*, p. 320 - 21. *The Principles of Ethics*, II, 211.

74. Daphne Simon, "Master and Servant," in *Democracy and the Labour Movement*, ed. John Saville (London, 1954), p. 160ff. Henry Sidgwick saw the difficulty that the courts would apparently not have laws to follow against unfair contracts and competition: *Lectures on Ethics* (London, 1902), p. 306.

75. Fike, p. 318.

76. In *The Principles of Psychology* (New York, 1899), II, p. 618, Spencer envisioned each citizen as defending "each other citizen's due sphere of action."

77. "Specialized Administration" (1871), *Essays*, III, pp. 420 - 23.

78. Peel, p. 79. The stomach analogy appeared in the most widely used cheap schoolbooks in England, those of the Kildare Place Society, the fourth book of lessons (1834): J. M. Goldstrom, *The Social Content of Education, 1808 - 1870* (Shannon, 1972), pp. 75 - 76, 100 - 03, 137.

79. Barker, p. 115. Spencer's friend Huxley had seen the logical weakness in Spencer's advocating individualism and no state-interference while he had compared society to a higher organism. In the latter, the units are all subordinated in systems of organs, and the central nervous system is dominant, like a government. Huxley's essay, "Administrative Nihilism" (1871), forced Spencer into his unfortunate revision of his analogy for industrial society.

80. Duncan, p. 493.

81. Robert M. Young, "Darwinism and the Division of Labour," *The Listener*, 2264 (17 Aug 1972), 203, 205.

82. Enid Gauldie, *Cruel Habitations: A History of Working Class Housing, 1780 - 1918* (London, 1974), pp. 118 - 20, 156. Peter N. Stearns, *Lives of Labour: Work in a Maturing Industrial Society* (New York, 1975), p. 87.

83. Young, pp. 204 - 05. In his study of American engineers and business

management, Edwin T. Layton, Jr. finds that ". . .[Social Darwinism] was the chief immediate inspiration of American engineers, including [Frederick W.] Taylor": *The Revolt of the Engineers* (Cleveland, 1971), pp. 141q., 138.

Chapter Nine

1. In the United States by the end of 1903, D. Appleton and Company had sold 368,755 volumes in their authorized editions. Of English sales, Spencer estimated in 1886 that "the number sold in the two countries . . . did not differ much": *An Autobiography* (New York, 1904), II, 113n., 242q. Then come the sales of the many translations of his works.

2. *Autobiography*, II, p. 533. For Spencer's rate of profit—between thirty and forty-two percent on books published in England by Williams and Norgate—see *ibid.*, p. 241, and "Views Concerning Copywright" (1877), in *Various Fragments* (New York, 1898), pp. 22 - 23.

3. Spencer's estate was in excess of L7500: Alfred W. Tillett, *Herbert Spencer Betrayed* (London, 1939). Spencer's estate put him among the top one percent of English wealth holders—one of 180,000 persons over twenty-five: Paul Thompson, *The Edwardians* (London, 1975), p. 12. Conversion of 1903 pounds sterling into 1975 dollars: in 1903, £1=$5; a dollar in 1903 could buy what costs $10 in 1975 (compare prices in *New York Times* advertisements); so more than £7500 x 5 x 10=$375,000 . In pounds today, £7500 would be at least £45,000. The 1903 pound was close in value to the 1911 pound, which may be multiplied by 4 for 1950 values, and by at least another 1 for 1969 (and by another 1 since then, or £7500 x 6=£45,-000): John Burnett, *A History of the Cost of Living* (Harmondsworth, 1969), pp. 199, 297; cf. pp. 129, 132 - 33. For Spencer's publishing losses—a total of £4350—see *An Autobiography*, II, 158, 415.

4. After his death, Spencer's collection was deposited in the British Museum Library and the Library of the London School of Economics. A list of translations is in Jay Rumney, *Herbert Spencer's Sociology* (1934) (New York, 1966), pp. 323 - 24. David Duncan, *The Life and Letters of Herbert Spencer* (London, 1908), pp. 129, 461. A Russian translator had to flee Czarist police: *An Autobiography*, II, 183 - 84.

5. M. Nagai, "Herbert Spencer in Meiji Japan," *Far Eastern Quarterly*, 14 (1954), 56. Benjamin Schwartz, *In Search of Wealth and Power: Yen Fu and the West* (Cambridge, Mass., 1964), p. 197.

6. Duncan, pp. 588 - 89.

7. (New York, 1948), pp. 203 - 04 (q. Spencer), 123, 215, 910 (q. Maudsley, who rephrased Spencer). Alistair Buchan, *The Spare Chancellor: The Life of Walter Bagehot* (East Lansing, Mich., 1960), p. 201

8. *Physics and Politics*, pp. 55, 214.

9. Duncan, pp. 411, 413. *Satan Absolved: A Victorian Mystery* (London, 1899), pp. 43q., 44, 38. The frontispiece reproduces George Frederic Watts' "Angel of Pity."

10. John I. Molloy, "Spencer's Impact on American Conservatism, 1870 - 1912," Doctoral dissertation, University of Cincinnati, 1959, p. 213. E. Digby Baltzell, *The Protestant Establishment* (New York, 1964), p. 99: "the dominant class ideology in America [in 1883] was to be found in the sociology of Herbert Spencer." Not all American conservative thinkers approved of Spencer: R. C. Bannister, " 'The Survival of the Fittest Is Our Doctrine': History or Histrionics?" *Journal of the History of Ideas*, 31 (1970), pp. 377 - 98.

11. *New York Times* (November 10, 1882), p. 5q. Beecher, "Poverty and the Gospel," in *Evolution and Religion* (New York, 1886), p. 299; also pp. 125 - 26.

12. Duncan, p. 305. Walter Troughton's "Reminiscences," Athenaeum Club Library, p. 45. Joseph Frazier Wall, *Andrew Carnegie* (New York, 1970), pp. 366, 390 - 91, 394 - 95.

13. Molloy, pp. 74, 88, 169. The Justices (and their terms) were Stephen Field (1863 - 97), his nephew, David Brewer (1889 - 1910), and Rufus Peckham (1896 - 1909).

14. Baltzell, pp. 165, 395n. Cf. Joseph Frazier Wall, "Social Darwinism and constitutional law with special reference to Lochner v. New York," *Annals of Science*, 33 (1976), 474, and David A. Hollinger's comment, 477.

15. Leopoldo Zea, *The Latin-American Mind* (1949), tr. J. H. Abbott and L. Dunham (Norman, Okla., 1963), pp. 228 - 32.

16. Duncan, pp. 161, 292, 319 - 23. Nagai, pp. 57 - 58.

17. *Progress and Poverty* (1880) (New York, 1930), pp. 133, 139.

18. Richard Hofstadter, *Social Darwinism in American Thought* (Boston, 1955), pp. 215 - 16. Goldman, "What I Believe" (1908), in *Red Emma Speaks: Selected Writings and Speeches*, ed. Alix Kates Shulman (New York, 1972), p. 35.

19. James H. Billington, *Mikhailovsky and Russian Populism* (Oxford, 1958), pp. 30 - 32, q. *Essays* (New York, 1899), I, 31.

20. Nagai, p. 59. Schwartz, pp. 46, 56, 60, 111.

21. Chow Tse-tsung, *The May Fourth Movement* (1960) (Stanford, Calif., 1967), p. 348n. Lu Hsun, "What Is Required of Us as Fathers Today" (1919), in *Selected Works*, tr. Yang Hsien-yi and Gladys Yang (Peking, 1957), II, p. 65. Noting Plekhanov's and Lunacharsky's uses of Spencer, Maynard Solomon wondered about Spencer's influence on turn-of-the-century socialism in all countries: *Marxism and Art* (New York:, 1973), pp. 218, 143, 342.

22. *George Eliot*: John Goode, "*Adam Bede*," in *Critical Essays on George Eliot*, ed. Barbara Hardy (New York, 1970), pp. 27, 29, 36, 37. Cf. *Middlemarch* (1872), beginning of Chapter 27, and *The Principles of Psychology* (New York, 1899), II, 397. *Daniel Deronda* (1876), Chapter 42, Lilly's speech on "the laws of development." Albert J. Fyfe, "Contemporary Psychology in the Fiction of George Eliot." Doctoral dissertation, University of Chicago, 1951. W. J. Harvey, "Idea and Image in the Novels

of George Eliot," in *Critical Essays on George Eliot*, ed. Barbara Hardy (New York, 1970), pp. 154 - 59. Michael York Mason, "*Middlemarch* and Science: Problems of Life and Mind," *The Review of English Studies*, N. S., 22 (May 1971), 154 - 56. 165. *Thomas Hardy*: Florence E. Hardy, *Life of Thomas Hardy* (1928, 1930) (New York, 1962), pp. 205, 370. *The Dynasts* (1903 - 08) (New York, 1925), pp. 6, 7, 99, 344, 518, 524. Douglas Brown, *Thomas Hardy* (London, 1954), p. 21. Samuel Hynes, *The Pattern of Hardy's Poetry* (Chapel Hill, 1961), p. 40. William R. Rutland, *Thomas Hardy* (1938) (New York, 1962), pp. 56 - 58. Olive Schreiner: *The Story of an African Farm* (1883) (Harmondsworth, 1971), pp. 12, 172. *From Man to Man* (1873 - 1920) (New York, 1927), pp 155 - 57, 184 - 99. *Arnold Bennett: The Book of Carlotta* (1904) (New York, 1911), p. 13. On *The Old Wives' Tale* (1908) and *Clayhanger* (1910), see James G. Kennedy, *English Literature in Transition, 1880 - 1920*, 13 (1970), 265 - 73. *The Journal of Arnold Bennett* (New York, 1933), pp. 140, 263, 350, 395, *The Journals* (1933), ed Frank Swinnerton (Harmondsworth, 1971), pp. 138, 140, 143, 145, 156, 167, 168, 182, 186, 208, 209, 334, 335. *D. H. Lawrence: Sons and Lovers* (1913) (New York, 1958), p. 212. Rose Marie Burwell, "A Catalogue of D. H. Lawrence's Reading from Early Childhood," *D. H. Lawrence Review*, 3 (1970), 216. *Aldous Huxley*: except for height and hair color, the literary portrait is of Spencer, "Uncle Spencer," in *The Young Archimedes and Other Stories* (New York, 1924), p. 12. Less certain is Spencer's influence on Joseph Conrad: John E. Saveson, "Spencerian Assumptions in Conrad's Early Fiction," *Conradiana*, 1 (1969), 29 - 40.

23. *The Journals*, p. 192.

24. *Sons and Lovers*, pp. 219, 417, 419.

25. *The Young Archimedes and Other Stories*, pp. 20, 22.

26. *Archimedes*, p. 19.

27. *Archimedes*, p. 40. The nephew saw, as his uncle did not, that "no characteristic [was] incompatible with any other" in a person: *ibid.*, pp. 129q., 130. Huxley denied that the name "Uncle Spencer" had anything "to do with Herbert Spencer," and said that it "was suggested by a tiresome relative of a relative by marriage." But the significance of the name is inevitable. *Letters of Aldous Huxley*, ed. G. C. Smith (New York, 1969), p. 913q.

28. *Lafcadio Hearn*: Beongcheon Yu, *The Art and Thought of Lafcadio Hearn* (Detroit, 1964), pp. 242 - 43. Allen Edmond Tuttle, "Lafcadio Hearn and Herbert Spencer," Doctoral dissertation, Northwestern University, 1950. *Hamlin Garland*: Donald Pizer, "Herbert Spencer and the Genesis of Hamlin Garland's Critical System," *Tulane Studies in English*, 7 (1957), 153 - 68. George Howard Savage, "Synthetic Evolution and the American West: The Influence of Herbert Spencer on the Later Novels of Hamlin Garland," Doctoral dissertation, University of Tulsa, 1974. *Theodore Dreiser*: Christopher G. Katope, "*Sister Carrie* and Spencer's *First Principles*," *American Literature*, 41 (1969), 64, 75. *Sister Carrie*

(1900), (New York, 1958), p. 74. Donald Pizer, *The Novels of Theodore Dreiser* (Minneapolis, 1976), pp. 10 - 14.

29. *Jack London*: Richard H. Warner, "A Contemporary Sketch of Jack London," *American Literature*, 38 (1966), 379q. *Martin Eden* (1909) (Baltimore, 1967), pp. 95, 275, 236, 276.

30. *Jules Laforgue*: Warren Ramsey, *Jules Laforgue and the Ironic Inheritance* (New York, 1953), pp. 90, 235. *Leo Tolstoy: Anna Karenina* (1877), tr. Constance Garnett (New York, 1965), pp. 357, 818 - 19, 835 - 36. Anton Chekhov: "The Duel, " in *Seven Short Novels by Chekhov*, tr. B. Makanowitzsky (New York, 1963), pp. 14, 27, 30.

31. *The Resurrection*, tr. Vera Traill (New York, 1961), pp. 48q., 225.

32. "The Duel," pp. 52, 23, 89q.; also pp. 31, 82 - 83. Examples from coelenterata and mammalia were equally frequent in Spencer's biology; and the inner and outer tissues of the jellyfish were his analogue for the first social differentiation of masters and slaves: *The Principles of Sociology* (New York, 1898), I, 491 - 93.

Selected Bibliography

There is no definitive bibliography for Spencer. There is a workable "List of Herbert Spencer's Writings" in David Duncan's *The Life and Letters of Herbert Spencer*, pp. 577 - 87. Jay Rumney reprinted this list and prepared a list of "Selected Translations" and a secondary bibliography to 1930 in *Herbert Spencer's Sociology*, pp. 323 - 51. Only the most useful secondary sources are listed here. Many more appear in the "Notes and References."

PRIMARY SOURCES

The Proper Sphere of Government. London: W. Brittain, 1843.

Social Statics, 1851. Abridged and Revised Edition, 1892. New York: Robert Schalkenbach Foundation, 1954.

The Principles of Psychology, 1855. Second Edition, Vol. I, 1870, Vol. II, 1872. Third Edition, 1880. Two vols. New York: D. Appleton and Co., 1899.

Education: Intellectual, Moral, and Physical, 1861. Part I of *Essays on Education and Kindred Subjects*. London: J. M. Dent and Sons, 1911.

First Principles, 1862. Second Edition, 1867. Third, 1875. Fourth, 1880. Fifth, 1884. Sixth, 1900. Fourth Edition. New York: De Witt Revolving Fund, 1958.

The Principles of Biology, Vol. I, 1864, Vol. II, 1867. Revised and Enlarged Edition, 1898 - 99. Two vols. New York: D. Appleton and Co., Vol. I, 1898, Vol. II, 1900.

The Study of Sociology, 1873. Second to Seventh Editions, 1873 - 78. New York: D. Appleton and Co., 1900. Rpt. Ann Arbor, Mich.: University of Michigan Press, 1961.

The Principles of Sociology, Vol. I, 1876. Second Edition, 1877. Third, 1885. Vol. II, Part IV, 1879, Part V, 1882. Vol. III, Part VI, 1885, Parts VII and VIII, 1896. Three vols. New York: D. Appleton and Co., Vols. I and II, 1898, Vol. III, 1899.

The Man 'versus' the State, 1884. Edited by Donald MacRae. Baltimore: Penguin Books, 1969.

The Principles of Ethics, Vol. I, Part I, 1879, Parts II and III, 1892. Vol. II, Part IV, 1891, Parts V and VI, 1893. Two vols. New York: D. Appleton and Co., 1898.

Essays, Scientific, Political, and Speculative, First Series, 1857. Second Series, 1863. Third Series, 1874. Revised Edition, 1890. Three vols. New York: D. Appleton and Co., 1899.

Various Fragments, 1897. Enlarged Edition, 1900. New York: D. Appleton and Co., 1898.

Facts and Comments. New York: D. Appleton and Co., 1902.

An Autobiography. Two vols. New York: D. Appleton and Co., 1904.

Duncan, David. *The Life and Letters of Herbert Spencer*. London: Methuen, 1908. Includes Spencer's "The Filiation of Ideas," 1899. Pp. 533 - 76.

SECONDARY SOURCES

BARKER, ERNEST. *Political Thought in England from Spencer to the Present*. New York: Henry Holt and Co., 1915. Pp. 84 - 132. Reveals inconsistencies in Spencer's philosophy of politics.

BURROW, J. W. *Evolution and Society: A Study in Victorian Social Theory*. Cambridge: Cambridge University Press, 1966. Especially Chapter 6. Pp. 179 - 227. Outstanding analysis of the reasoning carried on by Spencer and Victorian anthropologists.

CARNEIRO, ROBERT L. "Introduction," *The Evolution of Society: Selections from Herbert Spencer's 'Principles of Sociology.'* Edited by R. L. Carneiro. Chicago: University of Chicago Press, 1967. Pp. ix - lvii. Valuable synthesis of Spencer's reputation, especially as a social scientist.

COLLINS, F. HOWARD. *An Epitome of the Synthetic Philosophy*. London: Williams and Norgate, 1889. Authorized by Spencer, this is a ten percent précis, in Spencer's words, of *First Principles, The Principles of Biology, The Principles of Psychology*, and parts of *The Principles of Sociology* and *The Principles of Ethics*.

FIKE, LOUIS BRUCE. "Despotism, Liberty, and Retrogression: The Political Philosophy of Herbert Spencer." Doctoral dissertation, Brown University, 1969. Full study of almost all aspects of Spencer's philosophy of politics.

HART, ALAN. "The Synthetic Epistemology of Herbert Spencer." Doctoral dissertation, University of Pennsylvania, 1965. Penetrating analysis of *The Principles of Psychology*, Second Edition, Parts VI and VII.

HOFSTADTER, RICHARD. *Social Darwinism in American Thought*, 1944. Revised Edition. Boston: Beacon Press, 1955. Especially Chapter 2. Pp. 31 - 50. Thorough survey of the range of Spencer's influence in the United States before World War I.

MACLEOD, ROY M. "The X-Club: A Social Network of Science in Late-Victorian England," *Notes and Records of the Royal Society of London*, XXIV (1970), pp. 305 - 322. Illuminating record of Spencer's professional contacts.

MACRAE, DONALD. "Introduction," *The Man 'versus' the State, with Four Essays on Politics and Society*, Edited by D. MacRae. Baltimore: Penguin Books, 1969. Pp. 7 - 54. Perceptive characterizations of the drift of Spencer's reasoning.

MOORE, GEORGE EDWARD. *Principia Ethica,* 1903. Cambridge: Cambridge University Press, 1959. Pp. 48 - 58. Classic and ungenerous dismissal of Spencer's ethics.

PEEL, J. D. Y. *Herbert Spencer: The Evolution of a Sociologist.* New York: Basic Books, 1971. The best study of Spencer's milieu and a mine of information and opinion about his social thought.

RUMNEY, JAY. *Herbert Spencer's Sociology: A Study in the History of Social Theory,* 1934. New York: Atherton Press, 1966. Critical study of the strengths and weaknesses of Spencer's social thought as they appeared in 1930.

THOMSON, J. ARTHUR. *Herbert Spencer.* London: J. M. Dent and Sons, 1906. The most careful study of Spencer by a biologist.

YOUNG, ROBERT M. *Mind, Brain and Adaptation in the Nineteenth Century: Cerebral Localization and its Biological Context from Gall to Ferrier.* Oxford: Oxford University Press, 1970. Especially Chapter 5. Pp. 150 - 96. Shows Spencer's contributions to the development of neurology and psychology.

Index

(Only major subjects are listed; topics and names for which there would be only one (or even several) entries do not appear here. Works of Spencer are entered under his name.)